Mother's Letters

Mother's Letters

Essays
by

Elizabeth Hampsten

THE UNIVERSITY OF ARIZONA PRESS
TUCSON & LONDON

The University of Arizona Press
Copyright © 1993
Arizona Board of Regents
All Rights Reserved
⊗ This book is printed on acid-free,
archival-quality paper.
Manufactured in the United States of America.
98 97 96 95 94 93   6 5 4 3 2 1
Library of Congress
Cataloging-in-Publication Data
Hampsten, Elizabeth, 1932–
Mother's letters / Elizabeth Hampsten.
p. cm.
ISBN 0-8165-1370-8 (acid-free paper). — ISBN
0-8165-1373-2 (pbk. : acid-free paper)
1. Mothers—United States—Correspondence.
2. Hampsten, Elizabeth, 1932–   . 3. Women—
United States—Biography. I. Title.
HQ759.H235 1993
306.874'3—dc20   92-40901
                                                CIP

British Library Cataloguing-in-Publication Data
A catalogue record for this book is available
from the British Library.

CONTENTS

Introduction
ix

1. The Double A Ranch
3

2. "Where Are You From?"
21

3. Mother's Letters
41

4. School
87

5. Children
121

6. China
151

7. Sarah
173

INTRODUCTION

How often I hear my father's voice bouncing off walls when I am talking, with all his stammerings and gropings for the one word that will do, until I have to stop and catch again the timber of my own voice. Or coming into a roomful of people, of a sudden I feel a surge of my mother's shyness. When my grown-up children visit me in places they have never lived, they manage without being told to find where things are around the house. My stern Grandmother Morris, to jar me into good behavior, used to say, "Remember who you are," although the rebuke sounded so snobbish I hardly considered what she might mean. I assume now that part of what she had in mind had to do with who one was in relation to whoever had come before and after, and in some respects, though possibly not exactly along her train of thought, the question interests me. It does not after all seem such a bad idea to try to locate myself among the gestures, the tones of voice, the shared stories, expressions, and quotations that somehow make up the landscape that identifies who one might be.

In the Emily Dickinson sense ("I am nobody, who are you?"), no famous worthies stalk behind me: doctors, lawyers, merchants mostly, no chiefs I know of, and a good many teachers. Genealogy has never interested me—we are a scattered family and I am not even acquainted with very many of my relations. Rather, I have a sense of being preceded and followed and at times accom-

INTRODUCTION

panied by an arresting collection of people, some tugging toward or away from one another, by turns comforting and insupportable. My youngest brother visited me once when there were children in and out, probably a mess of toys on the floor, and I trying to start supper. He looked around at what some might see as wreckage, and said the house felt like a house ought to, he was home. Whether we seek family or flee it, we surely feel in our bones the accumulation of infinitely small gestures. There was a grate on the living room floor in my mother's parents' house, where heat came up from the furnace underneath. You were not supposed to step on the grate, but it was directly in the path between my grandfather's couch and the dining room. Before every meal, when I walked with my grandfather to his place at the table, he would take one firm stride directly on the center of the grate. You could hear the furnace shake and see my grandmother's lips tighten. At the dinner table, my father had a way of clearing his throat and tentatively raising his hand and then his arm toward whatever object he wanted—salt, butter, salad bowl. One had to be alert to what he was reaching for, because the sooner his gesture was interrupted, the sooner calm would return to the meal. Signatures like these bind us together in family—all know their part.

These pages come from a collaboration between my mother and me, not unlike the meals we cooked together, the socks we mended, our best moments in each other's company. Mother's contribution consists of letters she wrote, not to me but to her own mother and father—letters about college, and life with my father in the foreign service and then on an Arizona ranch. Many were about me and my brothers and sister, or at least mentioned us, giving me now that top-of-the-stairs sensation of overhearing grown-ups talk (the letters are in my possession). Her letters so tightly weave in and out of the essays they have led me to that it has been difficult to keep to chronology or always distinguish quotation from reminiscence. To assist readers, therefore, this is a summary of the sequence of

INTRODUCTION

my parents' lives and mine: they met in Washington, D.C., where my mother, Elizabeth Lockwood, was working in the Library of Congress after graduating from Wellesley College, and my father, Shiras Morris, was attending Foreign Service School. They were married at my mother's home in Tucson, Arizona, then went to their first consular post in Guadalajara, Mexico.

In two years Shiras was assigned to Stuttgart, Germany, where I was born in 1932. He was then assigned to Marseilles, my brother Charles and sister Felicia being born in the United States on Mother's trips back from France. My father's last post abroad was Montevideo, Uruguay. In 1942 we returned from there to Washington, D.C., where Pancho, the youngest, was born, and Shiras worked in the State Department until he resigned. In 1945 the family moved to a ranch in Northern Arizona, near Ashfork. During our years on the Double A, Charly and I were sent away to school. Then I went to Wellesley for a year and finished college at Flagstaff, Arizona (now Northern Arizona University). After that for me came graduate school, first at the University of Montana in Missoula, then at the University of Washington in Seattle, where Richard Hampsten and I were married and our child Sarah was born. Richard and I went to Ohio State in Columbus to teach English in 1960; Stephen and Andrew were born there. Four years later we moved to Victoria, British Columbia, for two years, then to the University of North Dakota in Grand Forks, where David was born and Mary Ann adopted, and where I continue to live and work.

This account for the most part leaves out some of my own adult life: teaching, being married and later not, twenty-some years of living in North Dakota, investigating the state's women's history, various feminist, peace-related, and political activities, a little foreign travel—activities that do not strike me as primarily imbued with that special interconnectedness up and down and across the generations of birth that interest me at the moment. Nor have I said very much about my own children—much as I confess that of the people who have been important to me over the years, they are the most interesting of all—and little also about my sister and brothers or other contemporary relatives and friends, lest a piece of writing might place more definition on them than I mean to. Writing, or print at least, exaggerates permanence, and is in danger of implying that, for all time, someone is this or that, however they have been described. Even though anything I might say is no more than my own view, I would not want anyone I know privately to think I intended to jar the continuity of their life by an account in a book.

On the other hand, with no intention of dishonoring the dead, I need not worry that those who are gone will feel reined in in any future. Nor do I have reservations about quoting from interviews, journalist reports, or published biography, where presumably the subject has had a chance to some say in the writing. Nor have I qualms over writing about the years of childhood, because while most adults must feel they are connected to the child they have been, they need not remain entirely defined by that. My sister Felicia, for instance, when she saw my description of our living on the Double A Ranch, told me that reading the book aloud in the car on the trip west when she was six was not the first time she had read a book through; she had read several books by then, she said. I do not think that my implying otherwise should make any difference to her life now, and so I have left that page alone, because on the hot scratchy back seat of Shiras' Buick on the interminable trek from New York State to Arizona, my supposing—for the thirteen-year-old I was then—that it was her first time was all that made listening to days of *Suzannah the Pioneer Cow* endurable.

Much of this book was written during a two-year leave from the University of North Dakota, for which I am grateful to the university administration and particularly to Bernard O'Kelly, Dean of the College of Arts and Sciences. I spent the leave on the coast of Uruguay, in La Floresta, the first year in the summer house of Nora and Boyd Goodliffe of Buenos Aires. To their hospitality and to that of their sons and daughters, I owe a debt for allowing my daily life to be so very agreeable. I thank the editors of *Journal of the Southwest* for permission to reprint "The Double A Ranch" (Spring 1987, pp. 80–95).

Friends, as always, have been patient, encouraging, and provocative. In addition to those whose contributions should be obvious during the course of the essays, Bjorn Benson, Marcia O'Kelly, Martha and Jay Meek, Victoria and Michael Beard, George Frein, Robert Lewis, and Sherryl O'Donnell read and nurtured parts along, as have David, Mary Ann, Andrew, Stephen, and Sarah Hampsten. They might count these pages along with my letters to them.

Mother's Letters

The Double A Ranch

While riding horseback on the ranch one afternoon of the summer I was sixteen, I very nearly was struck by lightning. Storms come suddenly in Northern Arizona, and I knew one was close, but put off turning toward home. When a bolt hit the wire fence just yards away, it was as if we stood, the mare and I, in the core of an explosion of light. A little closer to the fence, and the lightning might have killed us both; less forbearance on her part, and she could have killed me. But neither happened, and when the mare unshuddered herself, we went on, sloshing through the downpour.

Although I was close enough to feel electricity through the trembling of the mare and to be properly frightened, it was the fence was hit, not we. Everything was light, as though bursting away from us and brighter than any noon. (I was not aware of sound.) I have thought of that ride through the junipers and cliff roses at other times when I felt that sense of being, by accident, just to the side of an event that belonged to someone else but caught me also in its force. I watch and listen—to my parents and brothers and sister, to my husband and our children, to friends and relations and people I work and pass the time with—and I sense the force of these personalities. They, and the places where we knew each other, have and continue to form me. It is as though I move, from time to time, within fields like the electrical one—fields of love, or sorrow,

6
THE DOUBLE A RANCH

or humor, or adventure—not necessarily meant to include me, but there I am.

For my family of parents and brothers and sisters, the eleven years on the Double A Ranch, just north of Ashfork, Arizona, were the major years of our being a family, and made "family" nearly synonymous with adventure. This adventure began in early June 1945, in an old Buick that my father, Shiras Morris, had managed to buy in spite of wartime scarcity; gasoline came thanks to coupons he had saved. I had just finished seventh grade, Shiras had resigned from the Foreign Service, and we were on our way to the ranch he and Mother had bought in Northern Arizona—partly to be nearer her parents who lived in Tucson, partly because "it would be good for the children," and partly I suspect because my father liked to do the unpredictable. We started out in Ardsley Park on the Hudson and were headed to our grandparents' house in Tucson. The woolen upholstery in the Buick baked all the way west. When I read *Grapes of Wrath* many years later, I realized why the book sounded so familiar—nearly the same car, the same breakdowns at the same stops, and the same Highway 66. We were not quite migrant workers, but I've thought we might have been. The journey was interminable, six of us imprisoned in the smell of hot gray wool, but the tall, bright hollyhocks along fences and hedgerows in Ohio astonished me, my first intimation that a roadway could be beautiful.

Shiras did all the driving, for Mother did not drive, but sat next to him in the front seat, enduring the journey in spite of four children. The youngest, Pancho, was two, given to throwing boxes of Pablum out the window. He was my parents' delight, named for my mother's father, Francis Lockwood, and given the Spanish nickname to avoid two Franks in the family. By the time we reached the Rocky Mountains, my sister Felicia, or Fifi, had read her first book, all of it, out loud: *Suzannah the Pioneer Cow*. Fifi was six that year, Charly a year and a half older, and I thirteen. We scrapped and

7

THE DOUBLE A RANCH

whined and were thirsty and bored all those slow days across the continent.

A book about a dog named Fifi explained our lives before that summer's migratory journey. What made *Fifi* particularly ours, besides the name, was the fact that its characters, like our family, had "led a foreign service life, / in a house with a verandah, / and a poodle in Uganda." To be sure, that elegance was more exotic than any we had experienced: "Fifi the poodle mostly sat in, / a bed of eiderdown and satin, / and twice a day she chased the cat, / up and down the cocoa mat." Still, the dog had led a life we knew. Eleven years in consulates and embassies, all in beautiful cities— Guadalajara, Stuttgart, Marseilles, and Montevideo, although none in Uganda—had been enough for my father. Someone asked him once, what it never would have occurred to me to ask, why had he gone into the foreign service? Because it looked like "a useful and romantic thing to do" had been his answer. In this new venture, expertise he did not claim. Shiras knew nothing of country ways, had rarely been on a horse, and had not seen Arizona since his wedding. As a college freshman, my mother had ridden World War I cavalry horses in equitation classes at the University of Arizona in Tucson, where her father taught American literature. That was about the extent of their practical preparation for ranch living.

We arrived in Tucson at last in time for Pancho's second birthday on the second of July, and then made our way north, reaching Prescott by nightfall, after grinding the increasingly unwilling Buick up the hairpin turns of Yarnell Hill. Not knowing that on the Fourth of July Prescott celebrated its Pioneer Days, we found ourselves in the midst of massive festivities. Every lodging place had a "no vacancy" sign, so Shiras drove to the police station, confident, he told us, that the Prescott police would not want vagrants on its streets. He was right. We were directed to a room, a dormitory really, at the Fray Marcos Hotel, on the square, on Whiskey Row, next to the Palace Bar—names we thought belonged in cowboy songs. We slept on straw mattresses and brushed our teeth at a sink in the janitor's closet, thinking it a lark and another instance of our father's ingenuity. Mother, I expect, was less charmed.

We had better luck in Williams, somewhat higher and cooler in the mountains, and twenty miles from the ranch. We must have spent about two weeks in the little motel cottage among the pines, certainly a relief to Mother, who ever after said something grateful whenever we drove past the place on the way to town. The ranch was divided by a high sandstone ridge, the lower part only two or three miles from the town of Ashfork, a railway stop on the Santa Fe. Mother's sister and her husband, our Aunt Mary Margaret and Uncle Bill, lived in a house they had built on this lower section of the ranch, and it was Uncle Bill who was to be my father's partner and his first instructor in ranch management. Uncle Bill had grown up in Canada, had gone to the University of Arizona College of Agriculture, and had married my mother's younger sister. He had managed a number of ranger stations around the state when he and my father agreed to join in a ranching venture. Uncle Bill had stocked the Double A with Hereford bulls and half-wild cows from Mexico, an experiment in bargain breeding with limited success. (Shiras spent years rounding up the last of those Mexican cows.)

The Double A is one of the older ranches in that part of Arizona. Where we were to live was in the center of its two sections, divided by a fence that pastured cattle in the northern half in summer and in the lower southern canyons in the winter. Near the house was a sandstone dam (this was in the midst of sandstone quarry country) that was said to be one of the first dams for miles around, and reputed never to have gone dry. The house consisted of two rooms of hand-cut sandstone that we used as living room and bedroom, with window sills more than a foot deep. Attached was a frame kitchen, a shack really, moved from the other side of the dam. The house had six doors to the outside; Shiras replaced one with a window, and built on a large room with a fireplace as a

9
THE DOUBLE A RANCH

bedroom for my mother and himself. The two boys had the sandstone bedroom and my sister and I the separate frame bunkhouse with a tin roof, truly alarming during thunder storms. Juniper trees grew everywhere—they were considered weeds destroying rangeland—and particularly enormous ones brooded over and cooled the house. The house faced south, to the road that led eighteen miles to Williams; in back to the north was the spillway from the dam and a ravine with cliffs and grapevines and Indian petroglyphs scratched on sandstone slabs. Across the dam rose Home Again Mountain, for when we saw its volcanic palisades, we knew we were home again. (A similar promontory to the west was called Mad Woman's Lip, because a mad woman was said to have "lipped" off of it.)

Shiras worked prodigiously on the place to make it habitable, for it had been a long time since the Double A had been used for more than a camp at roundups, and he did most of the work alone. He built the fireplace and chimney, and in the large bedroom laid a floor of sandstone slabs, on which every Saturday in hot weather Mother sloshed buckets of water, sweeping it about on the stones, and then she'd sit in her chair and read or sew, grateful in the cool. We were a family adept at moving—the same green-and-white leafy curtains and wooden rings had shaded several sets of windows—but my parents had never before had to do so much to make a place livable.

The privy was a short walk by the fence, and kept clean with ashes from the stove. Clean water was hauled from town in fifty-gallon barrels, the bucket for drinking water always on the table by the kitchen door. In deference to sanitation, no one was allowed to drink out of the bucket dipper, but there was only a single cup next to it to pour a dipperful into. That first summer, Shiras rigged up a system of running water for the kitchen sink, and installed a shower and flush toilet in the lean-to off the kitchen. He pumped muddy water from the pond the dam made, and dug a septic tank that drained behind the house where he tried with not much success to grow vines. Some years later he built a large garage with a tin roof that drained water into a storage tank, and stopped hauling drinking water. His inventiveness seemed magical to us; he found solutions to nearly every necessity and inconvenience. The butane gas refrigerator came years later; we started with a rain barrel full of water in which Mother floated eggs, milk, and the pot roast she cooked the first day home from market. That worked well unless things sank, and then Charly was dispatched to the bottom to retrieve the goods. For all of us this was not just another move, it was a novel way of life—like camping, we might have said if we had ever camped. For Pancho, toilet training became a wholly unconstricted adventure—he had all outdoors. One afternoon the tree he picked was farther from the house than Mother wanted to follow him to, and she suggested that a nearer one might do: "Papa will fix," Pancho said.

Little by little things did get fixed. I helped paint the rooms, all of them white. The furniture from our parents' foreign service life may have looked odd in this rural setting, but to us it made things home. The curved sideboard with the sheet of glass on top; my father's victrola from his room at college; the wing chair; the desk with the secret drawer (postage stamps were kept there); the smooth, curved, rather art-deco bedstead; the spool beds—all these had been shipped during the war from the last post in Montevideo. Mother loved this furniture, and the houses, I think, where it had stood, and she dusted and polished and cared for it as best she could in the heat and grit of the ranch.

Outside along the front of the house we built a low wall of sandstone blocks from a shed that had been taken down—each of us assigned a daily quota of stones to carry. Mother planted zinnias along the wall, and for years we hauled buckets of water to them in the evening. A hop vine clung improbably to the kitchen overhang and thrived on dousings of dishwater. More sandstone slabs went to a terrace against the north side, the coolest place in

THE DOUBLE A RANCH

the summer, with a Virginia creeper that spread bravely against the stone house. I'd sit on the steps to read by the last of the evening light. There was even a swing from a branch of the juniper tree against the kitchen. The bunkhouse we whitewashed—you could see through the knotholes and between some of the better-warped boards—and we decorated the four corners of the roof with deer antlers, pagoda-like. Against the side that faced the house, we hung an elegantly bleached horned cow skull.

Though the house was the main thing for us children and for my mother, of course there was more. There was the barn, for one—hay, tools, odd bits of machinery, saddles, and the sign on the door from the Department of Labor, *Aviso a los Empleados* (Notice to Employees), warning against industrial accidents, in two languages. Log corrals, the uneven sides much higher than we were, looped against the back side of the barn, where children could sit on the top rails watching a branding, a butchering, or a corral full of frantic wild horses that had been rounded up in the canyons. Behind the barn I milked the domesticated range milk cow, Antilles, her offspring in successive years named Lesser Antilles. I had learned to milk goats on my grandmother's farm in New Hampshire, where we had been sent in the summers to relieve my mother of us for a few weeks, and as I was the only member of the family who knew how to milk, I set myself up on one side of the cow with a bucket, and Lesser Antilles provided competition on the other. As often as Antilles did not knock me or the bucket over, we had a quart or so of milk a day. Mother sometimes even coaxed butter out of a small glass churn from Sears. But she put her foot down about chickens—they were noisy, and dirty, and stupid, and a tyranny, because once you started, you could never leave the premises. She would not have them.

Horses were indispensable to the work of the ranch, and I became not able to imagine a horse existing except to work. Our horses were fairly ordinary range animals. A brown-and-white spotted one my father liked to ride had been poisoned by locoweed and would tear off through the brush when a fit struck. A steadier horse, Mutt, was considered safe enough for children; he was old and came with the ranch. Mutt had been a first-rate cow horse, and by the time he was relegated to carrying me around, had a lot to teach. I was allowed to ride with the men, which meant starting early in the morning before it got hot, and riding until midafternoon, when it was very hot. We'd move cattle from one watering place to another, or gather calves for branding, or check fences, or, when my father replaced the original herd of Mexican cows with more conventional Herefords, stalk, and coax, and sometimes wildly chase long-legged, long-necked aging cows, no longer encumbered by calves, up and down rocky canyon sides. Mutt never flagged, even though I might have.

One of Mutt's and my adventures became legend. The pond against the dam below the house was open to the range, and also watered the animals confined in the corrals at the barn. But when the water got low, there was no way to keep horses and cattle from wading beyond the run to the corrals and escaping. In order to separate two parts of the pond, a strand of barbed wire was needed across the water, but the pond never went dry enough for anyone to walk across to place the wire. Then someone had the bright idea that we could swim a horse across the tank and drag a strand of wire to the other side. But no one volunteered—cowboys do not get wet if they can help it—so Mutt and I gave it a try. I looped the end of a rope to my elbow, tied the other end to the wire, and held on bareback to Mutt's neck. The drag on the wire nearly pulled my arm, and me, off the horse, but we reached the other side, and it made a good story when anyone wondered how a wire had come to be placed across the water.

"The ranch" also meant the men who worked there. The Double A was of a size to need two men, and two or three more at roundups, these usually recruited in a quick tour of the bars in

13

THE DOUBLE A RANCH

Williams and Ashfork. But to hire his full-time assistant, my father took great care. He found Richard Bargeman—we children called him always Mr. Bargeman—who had developed cowboying to an elegant profession. He was soft-spoken, and kindly, and infinitely patient with animals. A small house was built for him, and his wife Leona and two little girls lived there. Before coming to the Double A, he had been an agent on the Navaho reservation, and Leona a nurse at the government hospital in Kayenta. He spoke Navaho, and taught us to count to ten. Mr. Bargeman was doubtless bemused by the vagaries of our family. Before his own house was built and his family joined him, he ate meals with us, he and my father at opposite ends of the table in the kitchen: mother and I sat on one side, Charly and Fifi on a bench against the wall, and Pancho on my father's lap, eating off his plate. Mr. Bargeman was full of stories about a roundup of wild cattle that had lasted for years on a ranch called the Hashknife. These tales, their names of places and people, took on the quality of mythology.

It was from Richard Bargeman that Shiras learned how to work a ranch, and learned also what he did not have to know how to do: he never roped. Roping was skilled and delicate work; it also was very competitive among those who did it well, and could be dangerous for those who did not, so he wisely left roping to Mr. Bargeman, who even enjoyed goat-roping competitions in town on Sunday afternoons. It was Mr. Bargeman who found a young quarter-horse mare for me, and brought her home without my parents' really deciding whether or not I should have more than a child's horse. She was named Coco. Mr. Bargeman broke her before I got home from school for the summer, but he never persuaded her to give up bucking, so my riding days often included tempestuous dumpings on the rocks. His professionalism about cowboying was wonderful to watch, and I wanted to see it all. We'd talk about what a "real" Western movie might be if anyone bothered to describe the truth; how close to move behind a cow and calf; how to know if your horse was getting tired; and mostly how to watch and listen and see "signs" of what animals had gone through the brush and how long ago. Day after day I rode with him, sometimes entire days with hardly any conversation.

My parents' cosmopolitan habits softened ranch living, and they were not so wedded to Western ways not to be willing to try things a little differently. Cowboys liked to set off early in the morning, ride all day, and then have a meal whenever they got home. There was no telling when that might be, but they expected chili and beans, or a pot roast, pie for dessert—a full meal at any hour. A few weeks of that, and Mother put her foot down as she had about chickens. She made sandwiches for my father and whoever was with him to take along, and served dinner at six o'clock. Shiras liked onion sandwiches—they were thirst-quenching, he said— and with fresh bread and Mother's mayonnaise, they might have brought back embassy receptions. Mr. Bargeman, and other men who scorned taking along even water, soon were deploying cans of coffee and coffee pots at the various watering holes where they were likely to find themselves at noon, to go with the sandwiches. ("You'd be surprised how little water it takes to make good coffee," was one of Mr. Bargeman's verities.)

Shiras, too, took a practical view. Western saddles are very heavy, and expensive, and he knew his children would not be able to lift them to saddle a horse for themselves. So he bought each of us a government-surplus, McClellan army saddle left over, I suppose, from the earliest days of World War II, when horses, somewhere, had been in use. McClellan saddles were certainly cheap—$15—and light, but they amounted to no more than leather wrapped around the saddle tree. There was a slit in the middle and a slight rise in front and behind, but not much to hold on to if you were falling off.

Shiras also bought a surplus army Jeep, then as un-Western as the saddles. He loved automobiles. He had had a Porsche in Europe;

when I was very little I rode on the shelf behind the single front seat, later in the rumble seat. There are photographs of Shiras in his white overall driving suit and aviator-like cap. The war and the move to the United States had brought to an end his pleasures with foreign automobiles, but he made up for that deprivation by not snapping onto the jeep the canvas roof and side curtains with the scratchy isinglass panels, except in very cold and rainy weather. He drove the jeep not only without sides or top, but usually with the windshield flat down on the hood as well. He once remarked to Mr. Bargeman, who would not have minded a little more shelter, that he had always longed for a convertible. "You have one," Mr. Bargeman said.

The Buick that had transported us from New York did not last very long. One of its late journeys was up the very steep and badly graded road from Ashfork, hardly more than a track scraped on top of sandstone rocks. The car stalled. Charly, Fifi, and I were told to get out and push. We lined up behind the car, and just before he let out the clutch, Shiras leaned out the window and said, "Watch it doesn't roll back on you." We pushed for dear life, and the car made it to the top of the hill, the three of us too witless to think of our father's control of the brake.

I learned to sew those summers, but because yard goods were hard to come by in the last years of the war, Mother and I cut up outgrown dresses and pieced them into blouses. We also became inventive with flour and sugar sacks, and one year I fashioned Shiras and Mr. Bargeman each a flour-sack suit, in a vaguely imitated cutaway design, to be worn at one celebration or other of family invention. One such event was graduation from Calvert School. Charly and I were sent away to school during the years at the ranch, but Fifi and Pancho learned at home with correspondence courses from the Calvert School of Baltimore, Maryland, until they went to the Verde Valley School in Sedona, Arizona. Fifi joined Verde Valley's first class, which helped construct the buildings and plan the school.

THE DOUBLE A RANCH

The headmaster, named Bret Hart and related to the writer, arrived at the ranch one afternoon (my parents had inquired about the school's admitting Fifi) just as Shiras, in Foreign Service dinner jacket, "boiled shirt" and black tie, was preparing to conduct Calvert School graduation exercises on the platform constructed for water barrels. Whatever Mr. Bret Hart's astonishment, he entered gamely into the festivities, and both Fifi and later Pancho attended Verde Valley through to their high school graduation. Our parents' penchant for wit and entertainment sometimes backfired, however. Among the men who worked at the Double A and sat at the dinner table telling of other ranches and the miles they had driven cattle, my parents gained a reputation for being arbiters of civilized living. But Mother once overheard Mr. Bargeman arguing with another man about whether one said "ingredients" or "ingrediments." Mr. Bargeman had corrected his friend because, he insisted, "Mrs. Morris always says ingrediments"—one of Pancho's expressions.

For me, in what were supposed to be the terrible teenage years, the ranch was wonderful. To be sure, there were hot, desperate, long afternoons of boredom when I stretched out on the bed and read all of Galsworthy, three trilogies in a single summer. My grandfather had ridden horseback with John Galsworthy when Galsworthy was on a lecture tour to the United States and found himself in Tucson. Galsworthy's thank-you note is tucked in a book of short stories. I read the miscellaneous collections of books my father's mother sent from Brentano's at Christmas: a critical biography of Sidney Lanier; the letters from Jane Mecomb and her brother Benjamin Franklin; histories of the cowboy; a book about Traveler, reputedly the first quarter horse, who had drawn milk wagons somewhere in New York state. (In college these books made my reputation as a near prodigy of the obscure.) I sewed, and did algebra by correspondence, and in the bunkhouse learned to play the

THE DOUBLE A RANCH

recorder to myself, I being the single nonmusical member of the family who was begged not to sing.

More often, I was out of doors, and whether working or hanging around afterwards, I found a great deal to watch and listen to. Karo Jim lived in a covered truck and would ask my father every few months to bring him a gallon can of Karo syrup (hence our name for him). Jim Bennett was a small, bowlegged man, who one thought of as very old until he began speaking of his mother, whom he supported and visited often. Jim Bennett had swum the Rio Grande when he was eight years old driving cattle with his father to Denver, and he had worked cattle ever since. All the cowboys deferred to him. His tales inevitably were cautionary, ending with Jim's tilting the back of his hat brim forward and saying, "I could have told 'em, and I did tell 'em"—implying too few took to heart what he told them, to their loss. He went to work on a large ranch owned by people my parents knew, where the Duke and Duchess of Windsor were entertained on their American visit. To show the royals a real cowboy, Jim was brought out and introduced: "Jim, this is the Duke and Duchess of Windsor." "Who-o-o?" Jim Bennett asked in a loud drawl.

Although Mother's desire to go to Arizona was the main reason for the move to the ranch, I think she was sometimes disappointed. She missed her friends, and she missed the more lively urban society of the Foreign Service posts. One winter when the snow was so deep it covered the top wires of fences, Mother did not leave the house pasture for three months, and when the Forest Service sent someone out in a snow-cat (a tractor-like vehicle) to see whether they were all right, she lost her temper because no one had thought to bring a fresh head of lettuce or even the mail. She did make trips to Tucson to see her parents now and then, and once in a while went to California or the East Coast to visit college friends. Whoever was in the house found her good company; the men were courtly toward her, but I fear she was lonely and bored. But she learned to cook better than she ever had abroad, when there were servants in the house and she was too shy to enter a kitchen. My best moments with her were reading aloud. She saved her mending for the summer, and we'd take turns darning socks and reading Henry James and Jane Austen novels one after another. When I read them now, I hear her and my voices in those books.

One Christmas Mother decided to give a party for the neighbors, meaning people living as far as thirty miles away. Mother was a genius at parties. She worked hard at making sure everyone had a good time, that the food was delicious, and that it looked as though she had nothing better to do than enjoy her friends when they got there. The party would be a noon luncheon, but grander than anything we children saw even at birthdays. She started several days ahead with roast turkey and ham, tomato aspic, and her inimitable mayonnaise, the oil gliding drop by drop from a cup in her left hand while with her right she beat a single egg yolk with a fork. There were Parker House rolls, cut and scored and buttered and folded over, and for dessert, mince pie and chocolate pie and very black coffee in her lovely, tiny coffee cups with doll-size spoons. She had us children well-trained at cleaning, peeling vegetables, and staying out of the way.

Those were her plans, and there may have been an extra trip to town to lay in supplies. It had been snowing and cold; then the weather warmed and it rained the day before the party. That morning was warm and sunny, and the roads were deep ooze. The jeep could not have reached the gate in underdrive. However, there was always the chance that someone might come, our nearest neighbors, for instance, on horseback. And, Mother reasoned, if anyone went to all that trouble and there was no party—well, she could not imagine the consequences. So all morning we finished slicking up the house, got out the damask table cloth, the white china with the silver rim, the crystal water glasses and cut-glass wine goblets. The

THE DOUBLE A RANCH

aspic quivered beautifully, the smell of turkey and sage makes me hungry yet. Then, in our best clothes, we waited.

Promptly at twelve there was a whinny from the barn, and answering whinnies from not far down the canyon behind the house. We went to the edge of the flagstones where the mud began and would endanger our shoes, and sure enough, here came the couple who lived on the ranch six miles away, their horses lifting one hoof and then another through holes they were making in the road. It was a wonderfully festive Christmas party, and met, I am sure, all my mother's exacting standards of hospitality.

"Where Are You From?"

RIDING DAY AFTER DAY on the ranch was all I wanted to do, and in my mind's eye, I still am able to move through canyons and flat places as though I had a map. To the north the land sometimes opened into grassy valleys. After a rain, pentstemon and Indian paintbrush flowers came like drops of blood against the reddish earth. To the south were limestone hillsides with yellow roses and squawberry bushes with tart, bitter berries that Mother and I made into pies and jam. The Santa Fe railroad tracks made part of the southern boundary of the ranch. There was a railway section house named Corva, and near it sweat lodges used by the men who worked there. When a steam engine went past us once while we were mending a fence, my father said that might be the last one I'd see. There was dark and porous volcanic rock here, and clumps of tall pines, sometimes enclosing open parks. The Forest Service placed road markers wherever one dirt road crossed another, but mileage markers seldom added up. Every year I mourned the end of summer desperately, when I would have to go back to boarding school, comforted only by Mr. Bargeman's saying I was more useful than the cowboys they'd be hiring for roundup.

For me the years on the Double A, summers really, came at just the right time, and I was the right child for the experience, fascinated by it all and wanting to learn. Had I been male, I might have stayed and kept the ranch, I don't know. The temptation to marry a cowboy—the only way I could see of continuing there—was very great, but I must not have been quite as romantic as my father. (And I expect also I had sense enough to see that marrying a cowboy was not the same as being one, the wives I knew being even more confined to house and housework than my own mother.) As it was, I had had all the pleasures, the work, and the knowledge about ranching without the worry, surely a reason many children brought up on farms and ranches thrived and remember them so fondly, without having remained there.

While cattle prices always were low, the Double A did all right as a business, but once we children had left for school and college, I think the ranch seemed to my parents more an anxiety than a pleasure. The hot summer winds made everyone nervous; people hallucinated clouds, looking for rain. Mr. Bargeman left, victim again to the alcoholism that he could control only for a few years at a time. He had come home on horseback very late one night, left his horse saddled in the corral and walked sulkily to his house. I unsaddled and fed the horse, appalled, I remember, at what was happening, that ranch life was ending for us. The last summer there I came home to find that the Double A had been sold. I helped pack, and drove the pickup of furniture to Tucson, where my parents were moving. It had rained just before I reached the city. The desert was ablaze with flowers, and the air had that unimaginable freshness the desert takes on after rain. If nothing else, the ranch had given me a feel of land and landscape.

Indeed I realized at the Double A that people living in a place could form their identities in it, they could make themselves part of that place. I longed to participate in such alchemy, to belong, in some secret way, to the mountains and canyons and small towns of Northern Arizona. Some of Mr. Bargeman's relatives worked on the Santa Fe railroad, and when I'd hear them list section houses along the line, it was as though these residents were joined into the

"WHERE ARE YOU FROM?"

names. Such intimacy was exotic to me, seductive, but it did not take me long to realize I was not likely to achieve it. Nothing in my past had allowed such connections. The "Foreign Service life" did not permit very long residence anywhere; and in addition, I knew that while the Consular Service in Stuttgart had provided me with papers alleging I had been born "on American soil," it was no soil to stand upon. Yet those are merely happenstances, and even I could tell that belonging to a place had to be a deeper phenomenon. My mother would speak about Meadville, Pennsylvania, where she had been born and lived until she was eleven, with what sounded to me like a taking-for-granted proprietary attachment that partly identified her and that she would not loose. On a car trip to the East Coast in 1950, she and my father drove through Meadville. She wrote back that the town was much the same except for fewer trees in the front yard of the family's house and a gas station at the corner. It happened to be Baccalaureate Sunday, and the college faculty members were lined up in caps and gowns on the church lawn. It was "a special grace" to have seen it, she said.

My father, on the other hand, did not appear to me to think of himself as belonging anywhere in particular. He had grown up in Hartford, Connecticut, a town he always mocked, once pointing out to my mother an entire magazine page of Miss Reingold contestants from Hartford and saying, "Now you see why I didn't marry a Hartford girl." We children called him by his name, Shiras (he was named for an ancestral Scottish judge), as though, I now wonder, he appeared hardly to have familial identity either—we would not have dreamed of calling him Dad or Father. (He complained once that "Shiras" did not show much respect, so for half a day we imitated stories in *St. Nicholas* magazines of Mother's we'd been reading and addressed him as "Governor," until he called it off.) Certainly there were places that drew him, particular ridges and valleys he'd ride out of his way for on the ranch, and he loved the city of Guadalajara, where he was assigned his first consular post,

"WHERE ARE YOU FROM?"

and where he returned in old age. But he did not appear to me to absorb his identity from any particular location.

Such a question of "belonging" to a locale I do not suppose would have occurred to me had my family not ever returned to the United States. In our first two or three years in this country, I could not have felt more a foreigner; it took me weeks to realize that a school "notebook" was nothing more complicated than a copybook, or *cuaderno* as we called it in second and third grade at the Crandon Institute in Montevideo. Montevideo must have been my Meadville, where everything I knew was orderly, in exquisite peace. The school I went to gave instruction half the day in Spanish, the other half in English. I could go up and down the aisles in the classroom and name every child: Felicia and Alicia, both with ringlets and each other's best friends; Jaime ("James" in English, I realized years later); red-haired Gloria and the rest. There were highly competitive jacks and rope-jumping on the playground, and roller-skating in formation to music in the basement gymnasium. The second grade provided the corps of angels for a school production of "Hansel and Gretel." Initially, and sensibly enough given my inability to carry a tune, the chorus did not include me; but when one of the angels took sick, I was put in her place. Those details are in Mother's letters to her parents; I remember only the bliss of wings and pink chiffon. One year I carried the American flag for a Fourth-of-July program, something that in Latin America can hardly now be the pure festival it was then. Our family left Montevideo in 1942. On the way to the port to board the night ship across the Rio de la Plata to Buenos Aires, we took Juanita home. Of all the people who had worked in our household, she was the one I felt closest to. We left her with her boxes in front of her house on the paving. While the taxi drove away through the narrow dark streets of Montevideo, I could see out the back window that she was waving. I felt sad in a new way for these endings. I would not see Juanita again, nor a way of life that had been so entirely satisfying to me.

"WHERE ARE YOU FROM?"

To my delight, almost fifty years after that departure I am again in Uruguay, this time by myself, on leave from university teaching. I live in the summer house of the family of acquaintances, in a seacoast town, an hour and a half by bus from Montevideo. I arrived in midwinter. The village is on sand bluffs above miles of beaches, dunes, pine and eucalyptus trees, and small tidy houses nearly all empty this time of year. Besides shopkeepers, I seem almost the only inhabitant; a few summer people come on weekends to putter in their yards, their children turned loose on bicycles. The house I am borrowing is constructed against the heat of summer, with concrete walls, tile floors, lots of windows and a wide veranda that ensures the sun does not reach into them. By what I'm used to, this is hardly winter, and I enjoy devising schemes against the noticeable chill.

The only English I read is what I write myself (along with letters from friends, to be sure), or hear from the BBC Worldwide Service on the shortwave radio. It is an extraordinary experience, this respite one usually only dreams of. It comes after twenty-some years of living in the same house, in Grand Forks, and teaching in the same English department, at the University of North Dakota, longer than I have ever lived in any one place. Five children have grown and left home, although thirty years of marriage to my husband Richard have not matched this semblance of permanence. Returned from a year's teaching in Beijing, China, he had become so engrossed in that culture, I am supposing, that he could not continue supporting our two lives together. And so I find myself by myself, not always quite sure how to behave without a companionship that for me for so long had seemed firm and very rich. Right now, it suits me well to be a stranger, puzzling my way among a society that looks fixed and of long habit, with the stranger's privilege of exploring other people's haunts, and permission to be inept. North Dakota, lost at the top of the map, is a state that no one even wants to drive through if they can help it. Nevertheless, I prize living there. I have built friendships and enough familiarity with the state that I look forward to returning. Yet for now, it is a relief to be obviously from away; even living in someone else's house makes me feel at home.

The first time I left Uruguay, I was right to think that my own connections to the world would not again be as benign. Our family next lived in a Washington, D.C., suburb while my father worked at the State Department. As the new kid in school, I was asked, as children always ask, where was I from? I tried "Uruguay," but no one knew where that was, so I said I was born in Germany, which got me sent home for a note, the school authorities anxious about German spies. I settled on claiming New Hampshire, in deference to my grandmother's having had me and my sister and brother at her farm there for the summer. That satisfied inquiries on the playground, but the question keeps coming, until it has occurred to me that "Where are you from?" is a judgment to the effect that one is not "from" wherever the conversation is taking place. When I travel about North Dakota, someone is bound to ask where am I from, and they don't mean Grand Forks; outsiders are assumed to be on their way to somewhere else. To elect to live in North Dakota, and to make an effort to stay there, appears to the locals as somewhat unusual.

Thus to be "from" somewhere I have supposed must be a gift, like the ability to carry a tune, that comes irrespective of class, educational experience, or whether one moves often, or travels. It is not particularly connected to knowing the history, the topography, or the origin of place names, but comes, it is my guess, with a kinetic sense of space. In North Dakota people identify not the town they live in or near, but name the county. In Uruguay people locate a school, a town, or their bus stop at the kilometer marker on the highway radiating from Montevideo, where at the capitol building begins kilometer 0. To such a method of thinking, other kinds of place-name information must seem arcane. In North Dakota, I

"WHERE ARE YOU FROM?"

have yet to find anyone among classrooms of students or audiences in other towns I might be talking to who knows the origin of the name of the town of Carpio. But even as people smile while I tell them (according to a WPA state guide, the first post office was in a railway car, so one went to the Car P.O.), they know that they are the ones "from" North Dakota, and I am not. Speech certainly is one of the markings of the stranger, the person who does not sound quite right; speech can be the passport to a very particular identification. Richard, who feels his origins in Southern Illinois much as Mother did hers in Meadville, uses the phrase "in my dialect" to name variations he grew up with. In that sense, I cannot claim a dialect.

But certain regions attract me strongly, others I resist living in. The West draws me: the ranch in Northern Arizona, and Flagstaff where I went to college; Montana and Washington that gave me graduate school; and North Dakota where I feel I thrive now. To the East and Midwest I sense little connection. The New England landscape is beautiful, but my grandmother was too stern and dour for me to want to linger. The Hudson River Valley, where the boarding school was located, in the 1940s was tree-filled, but I desperately resisted being at that school. And the agricultural Midwest, the much-sung heartland of America, where Richard had his first teaching job at Ohio State, sunk me into faculty-wifery. I felt alien to those parts.

This attraction toward or alienation from places is certainly colored not only by topography and landscape, but by the people or events associated with a place. One's "sense of place," I would assume, is inevitably confounded or enriched or at least complicated by whatever social situations or elements of personal affection happen to go with it. For me, the Mississippi River makes none too removed a boundary from territories I do not really want to inhabit again if I can help it. That prejudice I know I owe to a disquieting attach-

"WHERE ARE YOU FROM?"

ment to my grandmother who lived in Hartford, Connecticut, and Concord, New Hampshire.

Grandmother Morris was rich as she was strict; she was generous, and she wanted to be kind. Every Christmas, in addition to the books, she sent a box of clothes; in it, my best dress for the coming year, smocked, of soft wools or flowered cotton prints. Cousin Ronny, at about age ten, one later Christmas when I was visiting her, put just right her benevolent and stern materialism. His father was trying to get him bundled up to go home. Ronny stood on the top step between the dining room and parlor, looking over the ravages of tissue paper, and said, "Well, Grandmother, it certainly has been profitable." She welcomed us to her house in Hartford when my parents made their sporadic holiday leaves to the United States from distant consular posts. I remember a party she gave—I must have been about five and Charly and Felicia stairsteps beneath me—that still holds one of the exquisitely tactile moments of my life. The three of us discovered the silky black velvet, and very large, behind of one of the guests. Close together in a row we stroked that vast and soft posterior. How Grandmother carried off the rest of the evening after spotting us, I cannot think.

Facts, in this part of the family, are hard to come by. One fact nobody knew was Grandmother's age. She would not tell, and not even her children—my father, his younger brother (our Uncle Judson), and their sister (Aunt Grace)—knew how old she was. Oddly, I was the one to find out. In 1950, a census year, I happened to be with Grandmother in Hartford during a holiday from college when the census forms arrived. Grandmother was in bed with sciatica, which troubled her severely, and she told me to fill out part of the forms. An item asked for numbers of rooms in the house. There was a lovely circular staircase, and rounded hallways at either end; bedrooms had dressing rooms; there were pantries and maids' rooms. I called a "room" anything with four walls, a door and a window, and counted seventeen. Grandmother was furious. This was a small

"WHERE ARE YOU FROM?"

house, taxes would ruin her, how could I be so stupid? When she folded the forms and sent me to mail them, because they were not in an envelope, I could read the top lines by forcing the bundle into a tube. That was how I learned that in 1950 Grandmother was seventy-seven years old.

The least mysterious fact about Grandmother Morris was her being rich. The wealth was largely of her own making, and had begun with a small hardware manufacturing plant in Hartford that her husband left her when he died. She invested money cannily, into the Ford Motor Company when few thought that automobiles had a future, and into the Xerox Corporation at a similarly dubious time in its beginnings. She spent her mornings on the telephone at a small table in the upstairs hallway in conversation with her broker, Charles Cooley of the Connecticut Bank and Trust, names I still remember.

During the three summers of our family's years in the East before the move to Arizona, Charly, Fifi, our cousins Jay and Ronny, and I stayed at Dingleton, Grandmother's estate in New Hampshire. These summers elevated Grandmother from a mere distant sender of packages to an emphatic presence in our lives. Dingleton had been a farm once, on a wooded hill almost directly across the Connecticut River from Windsor, Vermont. Even the drive from town was dominated by Grandmother's force: from the highway that follows the river, she would cut into the wooded side road, rushing her station wagon in high gear up the very steep gravel road and shifting without stalling just before the first hairpin turn. Before long the road opened onto a meadow bound by a log fence, where her horses grazed, the banks on the upper side of the road heavy with blackberries. A little farther, the land opened again, enough for a large house, and gardens, barn, and pastures. You can walk beyond the edge of the vast lawn behind the house, where grass is cut for hay, and down a short but darkly shaded path to a lookout among the trees for a view of the Connecticut River and the White Mountains of Vermont. In early summer, there are strawberries underfoot.

After its time as a farm, Dingleton had been bought by two women who took summer art lessons from the painter St. Gaudens, who lived on the next estate on the same steep hill. The women had designed Dingleton's Georgian house, its pillared veranda supporting grapevines, its large kitchen, pantry, dining room, hallway, parlor, and what was referred to as the billiard room. From there (the room now is lined with books), a corkscrew staircase, where children were not allowed, led to Aunt Grace's bedroom and then down a long hall past Grandmother's room and two guest rooms. The back stairs led to a series of little wood-paneled maids' rooms above the kitchen that were given over to us children during the Dingleton summers. A wide wooden staircase led from the center of the upstairs corridor down to the front hall, where stood the most distinctive memento of the St. Gaudens ladies, a female portrait bust carved into an oak post in the front hall. Polished bare breasts met one exactly at eye level—you could hardly avoid the object either coming down the stairs or approaching from the front door. The post was the subject of much ribaldry among us children, although we never heard a grown-up remark about it.

Dingleton harbored a multitude of livestock: eight or ten horses of highly bred dispositions; bantam chickens; two sheep; a herd of goats; pigeons; two Afghan hounds; several cocker spaniels; and stray barn cats. Except for occasional hired men, Grandmother and Aunt Grace took care of all these animals themselves. I adored Aunt Grace. She was in her twenties and only fourteen years older than I (and if anything, even more strict with us children than Grandmother). Grace rode in horse shows and taught, or tried to teach, us children to ride. There was a Shetland pony who rushed at clotheslines to rid us off her back, and a Morgan mare that regularly ran away with me, and when she returned to the stable in foams of sweat, it was up to me to walk her until she cooled off. I learned to milk goats. I cleaned out stalls, and herded goats to the vast back lawn turned to pasture, where I tied their ropes to stakes. The chickens were unrelievedly nasty. Two Russian wolfhounds were let out of their pen each evening, and if I had not found some excuse to be indoors, they invariably sought me out in bounding leaps and knocked me down.

How Grandmother and Aunt Grace managed such a conglomeration of animals, gardens, woods and fields, buildings and machinery, to say nothing of five children, still amazes me. Perhaps survival had to have depended on strict discipline. One afternoon while I was riding, the other children turned to hurling the bantam chickens over the chicken house fence to watch them fly. When discovered by Grace, they were chased with a buggy whip to the house, where Grandmother sent them to bed and fed them supper out of dog pans. Little wonder we were docile when returned to our parents. Mother wrote of one of these returns:

> The children have grown so—Bitsy [my nickname] 1½ inches since she went away, and Charly and Fifi each an inch. They have improved greatly too under their grandmother's tutelage and insist on making their own beds every morning and are so helpful and so happy about helping. They seem to have enjoyed their summer, but they're happy to be at home again too. They all have the fortunate dispositions of enjoying the present and the place where they are, and I don't think they are ever homesick, either for home or for Windsor.

Grandmother's passion was for the animals. Years before, driving through an industrial New England town, she had seen in someone's window a chicken trapped inside a bottle. Her outrage did not stop with berating the owner. She joined the SPCA and ever after used her barn and stables as hostelries for sick and injured horses and other livestock. At Dingleton, no animal was killed or left to die unattended, and some years the stables resembled an animals' retirement home. There was a moral edge to almost everything

Grandmother did, and with us children it was as though we were so in need of improvement she did not know when to stop. She took us for treats at the drugstore soda-fountain, but sneered at ice-cream flavors that were not chocolate, because, she'd say, they had no "character." Her scorn for people who chose strawberry was withering. Whenever she said to me, sternly, "Remember who you are," I knew that what she meant was I'd done something to disgrace her sense of who *she* was, for I was in trouble most of the time. Even during our earliest visits, in the garden in Hartford I'd lose my way among the long paths between clipped hedges that I could not see over or quite reach the ends of. I'd fall out of the high four-poster bed I was put into, and every night knew I was bound to awaken on the floor.

During the Dingleton summers, she liked to take us for drives in the wood-paneled station wagon that we termed a "banana wagon." There would be stops at historical markers, and if at supper we children could not name which Revolutionary general had done what at which site, we forfeited dessert. We played games naming state capitals; we learned the names of countries and their capitals and principal minerals. Children should know facts and stay out of trouble, she thought, and saw to it that we did both. The library room had a complete set of *Mother Westwind* books, and a "girls' series" set during the American Revolution. I read many years' of *The Readers Digest* and romantic novels like *A Lantern in Her Hand*.

When I was a little older than during the summers at Dingleton, I stayed with Grandmother in Hartford during school holidays. She lived by herself then, as Grace had married, and while Grace had only moved to West Hartford and visited nearly every day, Grandmother felt alone. It may have been that by now she thought I was old enough to listen, and in the city house there were not all the chores with animals and gardens to keep track of. In any event, Grandmother liked to talk, and these were my best times with her. She might be sitting on a kitchen stool after washing up the dishes

"WHERE ARE YOU FROM?"

or sitting by the small side table in the dining room next to the windows after breakfast (always oatmeal porridge because it "stuck to your ribs"), and she'd tell me about her children. There was my Uncle Judson, who had run off to college at Stanford; she still held it against him that he had gone so far beyond the civilized pale of the Connecticut River.

Her disapproval of my father rested largely on his having married my mother. Nevertheless, Grandmother was proud of Shiras, but I doubt she let him know. She told of how at college at Harvard he was to sing in a comic performance (it may have been "The Hasty Pudding Show"), and, forgetting lines to a song, made up others on the spot that were funnier than the original. She brought herself to tears telling of the time she went to his graduation to discover he was receiving honors and had not mentioned the fact. "I thought you'd expect it," was all Shiras had said. She visited him and my mother at his Foreign Service post in Germany, where others told her how kind he was and how good at his work. She told me these stories, I felt, rebukingly, as though I did not live up to him. She made people feel—my father and me especially—that we would never be able do well enough to suit her, but that her disapproval came mainly because she loved us more fiercely than any love we could return.

My last visit to Grandmother Morris was in 1963 (if my look at her census form was correct, she would have been ninety), when I was married and living in Columbus, Ohio. I took Sarah, the oldest of our then three children, along to show her off, but also for protection, I suspect. The visit did not go very well. Sarah, far from awed, ignored her great-grandmother and climbed on the furniture. Grandmother's angry conversation those days was directed against anyone who opposed Richard Nixon or had it in mind to run a freeway through her house (which as far as I know has not happened). She died not many months later, but her presence is not one I am likely to shake off.

"WHERE ARE YOU FROM?"

There was a reception one year given by the Virginia Woolf Society at the Newberry Library in Chicago. I went partly as an escape from the Modern Languages Association meeting in the Palmer House, where like hundreds of others who teach in college English departments, I was to read a paper. I had never seen the Newberry, the famous scholar's haven. It was winter, and raining in early evening, and I remember the light and opulence when I stepped inside the building—the high ceilings, dark wood, heavy furniture. The reception was in an upstairs room. There, women in long tweed skirts with uneven hems, wearing shawls or hip-length cardigans, were nibbling raw vegetables. Strange imitations, they appeared, of photographs of Virginia Woolf. The scents of sherry and moist wool and furniture polish took me away from literature and back to my grandmother's house and her severe instruction about the history and confirmation of Queen Anne chairs—forbidding me to sit on them.

But there was another more tangible trace of her here. Leaving the library, I stepped into a side gallery to admire the woodwork—bookcases with glass doors, carved arm chairs. Above the framed doorway of polished oak that I had come through was a portrait of a young woman in a rose Empire-style dress. Astonishing to me, the brass plaque identified her as the Duchess of Oldenberg, the name "Oldenberg" long fraught for me with mystery and scandal. The mouth and chin of the face in the portrait were exactly like my sister's, and the upper part, large eye sockets and high forehead, could have been my own. The painting looked to me like a prankster's combination of Felicia and me, and indeed might be, if the story I'd heard was at all correct.

Grandmother's parents had come from Germany, I'd been told, where her father was gardener to the Duke of Oldenberg. The family had arrived in the United States with more children than they could manage. Two infant daughters were placed for adop-

37
"WHERE ARE YOU FROM?"

tion; one, my great-aunt Ceceel, went to a family in New York, and my grandmother went to a family named Root in Hartford. It may well have been that the father of my grandmother was not the gardener to the Duke of Oldenberg, but the Duke himself, and that the parentage was a motive for allowing the little girls to be adopted. I know no more than that, but standing in the Newberry Library, it pleased me to suppose that the Duchess of Oldenberg with the somewhat bemused expression on her face might be a distant relation of mine.

An uncertain heritage this, whether royally connected or not. During each of my Hartford Christmases, there would come an afternoon when an elderly man appeared at the door carrying an enormous box of gladiolus. The flowers were for Grandmother, who would accept the box but not invite him in. He was her brother, she said once, and that was all. Grandmother was vain about her slim and narrow feet—a shoe salesman had said, she liked to tell, that she "didn't have feet, she had slivers." The feet of the bringer of gladiolus were very large, I could not help noticing, and the dark suit he wore was in the style of a European workman.

Grandmother had traveled to Tucson for my parents' wedding, and mentioned the Lockwood family always with respect, but she never visited us on the ranch. As I said, beyond the Connecticut River, her map was populated by monsters around its edges. But her niece, our Cousin Faith, did come during our fifth summer there. It was the occasion for Shiras making our first family excursion to the Grand Canyon, eighty miles away, which, he always assured us when anyone became impatient to see this natural wonder of the world, would still be there when we did go. Cousin Faith was the daughter of Grandmother's sister Ceceel, whom I remember as having a sanguine, even ebullient disposition. Cousin Faith may be even more cheerful and energetic than her mother. She was then curator of French eighteenth-century silver at the Metropoli-

"WHERE ARE YOU FROM?"

tan Museum as well as an inveterate world traveler. I think she and my father felt more closely drawn to each other than to any other relatives, and there were numerous trips she and my parents made together. She was full of enthusiasm for the ranch—on the day the two of us took a ride to a stand of flowering century plants on the top of a limestone ridge, she made me feel the sight was as spectacular as anything she had come upon in other continents.

I do not know why Grandmother should have been so angry at the world in general, but it makes me sad. She had her sorrows—her husband's death when my father was in college, and she spoke still of the event as though it had been recent. Sciatica troubled her always, a pain hardly conducive to cheerfulness, but I should not think circumstances alone altogether account for her unhappiness. When my parents became fed up with a fit of my bad temper and would say, "You are just like your grandmother," I felt very badly, although I know there are respects in which I do resemble her. I look like her, I am built rather like her. Like her, I can be fairly fierce, or so friends tell me. So, while I consider myself far from a discontented person, I think I have an idea that what drove her rages came partly from the strongest aspects of her character. Despite her conservative, not to say reactionary, politics, I can share her exasperation when things are badly done, or wasted, or when land and animals are mistreated. Grandmother Morris was a brilliant manager—of money, of her strange estate—and whatever she turned to was done with forbidding competence, traits I certainly admire. She was a wonder at wrapping packages—paper folded into sharp corners, string so taut it snapped. It was dangerous to be the one to place a finger where she tied the knot, but I am in awe of the hazard she created.

It was not only that she taught me to make my bed and wash my socks, but that for all her and Aunt Grace's exactitudes, work became interesting and worth doing ("well," they would have said).

"WHERE ARE YOU FROM?"

I learned to milk, to ride, to curry a horse, to clean out horse and goat stalls; I learned the names of the parts of the horse and what various straps on saddles and bridles are called. Grandmother paid us ten cents an oatmeal box for picking wild blackberries, and then I joined her in the jam-making, a production I still go through, every summer, wherever I am with whatever fruit is at hand. I would say that, at a ten-to-twelve-year-old level during those Dingleton summers, I became moderately competent in a few skills. I began to see the advantage of knowing how to do things, and it even dawned on me, although more slowly and through the murk of boredom, that a grasp of information could be useful. My impression is that Grandmother thought the world a dark and lonely place, where few were likely to be one's companions, and if anything was to be accomplished, you had best be prepared to do it yourself. Without subscribing to the whole of her dour vision, I feel sympathetic to the substance of her critique, enough to value competence and self-sufficiency.

She disapproved of our family's move west, and was disappointed in her expectations of me. As for me, I was least afraid of her in those moments when she was least anxious, or least in pain, and we'd be cooking jam or weeding a garden plot together, or when she would get into her story-telling mood, and a geniality and humor escaped her. When I listened to Leslie Fiedler's lectures in Montana on Hawthorne's novels, I realized that Fiedler was presenting the Puritanism of New England as though it were to him some distant anthropological rite. I said to him once that those people and their ideas were still there, and I had a grandmother to prove it. She was entirely New England (whatever that means), and I know that she is in my bones.

I expect one's sense of place is deeply psychic; I doubt we are moved by or drawn to mountains, deserts, rivers, woodlands, coast lines, or amber waves of grain alone and in a vacuum, but imper-

"WHERE ARE YOU FROM?"

ceptibly respond to them in combination with whatever human circumstances connect us to them. Hardly anything can be more lovely than the New England landscape—the view from the almost secret lookout beyond the lawn at Dingleton could grace a Christmas card—yet the briefest visit east of the Hudson renews my conviction that that is where medieval monsters lie.

Mother's Letters

After Mother died in 1970, Shiras handed me down from high in a storage closet the hatbox of letters she had written to her parents. I had not known of these letters, and was amazed there were so many of them, and was especially pleased that my father should give them to me, for he was not a letter-saver; he thought saving letters was impolite.

Mother's began in 1928 when she left for college at Wellesley, and they stopped in 1950, the year her mother died. Mother wrote to one or the other parent nearly every week, and sometimes oftener—about her daily routines, trips she and Shiras took together, friends and parties, books she read, children's doings. The letters say a good deal about her affectionate relationships with her mother and father. I began to browse here and there among the years and postmarks: Guadalajara; Stuttgart; Marseilles; Montevideo; Williams, Arizona. There was her perfect "library hand" in even loops up and down, learned during her Library of Congress job after college—describing skiing trips in the Alps, summers on the beach in Uruguay, roundups on the Double A—life from a different view than the discontent and sadness one sometimes felt around her. It was hard for me to read many pages at a time. I happened on her telling of a tea party some weeks after I was born: "One of the ladies at the tea begged to be taken to see the baby, and she clasped her hands and gasped and sort of goggled in wonder

44
MOTHER'S LETTERS

and finally said, 'My God, how beautiful.'" I stopped reading there, and put the letters back in their hatbox on the top shelf of my own clothes closet.

Now, after nearly twenty years, I *have* read them, not too sadly to enjoy again Mother's wit, her kindness, her pride in us children, and the interesting life that she and my father had in the Foreign Service and ranching in Arizona. I read them too trying to fathom better what the letters meant to her and what part writing them had in a life of hers separate from children. All of us knew her letter-writing was important, if only because keeping up correspondences was what you were supposed to do. I never wrote home often enough, so it was easy to suppose that at least she was discharging obligations. (Mother begins once: "To quote Bitsy's immortal words in her last letter from Windsor, 'I have not written to either of you for so long, that I feel that I should write to you both at once.'")

In whatever house we lived in, and especially at the ranch, my parents' bedroom was Mother's room in the daytime, with her desk, comfortable chair, and good light, so that when she went to her room with a cup of coffee and closed the door, we knew that would be the last we'd see of her for a while. She would read, play solitaire, take naps, and write letters, and was not to be disturbed. (In my own household I too made a habit of closing the bedroom door, book in hand. Soon I'd hear, "Where's Mom?" downstairs, and one child going to the basement, another to the backyard perhaps, and then footsteps up the stairs and down the hall and a knock, and "Hi! Mom.") Mother, I now think with only a little exaggeration, did not go to her room to write letters so much as she wrote letters so she could go to her room. She described from the ranch one of those retreats:

> We are being honored this evening by a visit from our rock-quarry neighbor, Mr. Brown. He is a very nice man, but he seems to be in a

very elated state this evening, so I left him to Shiras, Richard, Hutch, Pancho and Fifi, thinking they would be enough to listen to him, and sought sanctuary in my room to write to you. His conversation, when he's "been to town," is of a nature highly interesting but unsuitable to the ears of children. I daresay Pancho and Fifi are enjoying themselves.

Certainly the letters were important in her relationship to her parents. In the early years of college and her first move or two, her parents sustained her with advice and encouragement, and as the years went on, the balance reversed and Mother was their support through old age. But in addition to such familial reasons for writing, I have to suppose that Mother was writing because she wanted to *write*, and letters to her parents were the available vehicle, something she did that was separate from obligations to her own household, or even to her parents for that matter. There was a portrait photograph of her that hung above my grandfather's couch in his study, taken probably when she finished college. She is kneeling, in profile, in a long satin gown draped off the shoulders, hair cut short in the style of the twenties—very beautiful and a little wistful. I have always thought that is how she and those who knew her thought of her, "before you children came along" as the relatives used to say. That was her vision of herself as herself, and I expect she best kept it up in the letters, where the voice is bright, intelligent, even now and then sounding to me a little posed. To be sure, she is relating a life largely circumscribed by others—my father's Foreign Service career, her children, the duty she felt toward her parents. Nevertheless I think that another life, more of her own, shows up as well. For one thing, so many passages do more than it would take to send information or satisfy the requirement of letters home. When she describes Meadville and Oracle in answer to a query from her father, Mother evokes for me both her attachment to these places and the attachment of the family to each other:

46

MOTHER'S LETTERS

You ask me, Daddy, what the happiest period of my childhood was, that I best like to remember, and that is very easy, it is when we were in Meadville. I don't remember ever being anything but happy there, except the time the oak tree was cut down, and one other day when I came home from school and Mother was sad because Grandpa Pritner died, and then it was pretty awful while she was away and nothing seemed to go right, and once or twice Sister and I had perfectly dreadful quarrels, but aside from those few times, it's hard to think which of my memories is the nicest—long mysterious exciting walks with you, or playing Ladies with Mother, or leading my outlaw bands around with bows and arrows, or playing on the campus, or in the snow, or in the leaves in the fall with you, or what. That summer in Oracle was great fun too, when we named our walking sticks so grandly, and I first learned to ride horseback, and we explored about on foot, and Mother's visits were such festive occasions. That was a lovely summer. I think I won fifth prize in a sewing contest, too. I was very proud of that, although I'm sure there were not more than four other contestants.

When our family lived in Marseilles, in the mid-1930s, the subject of writing itself enters the correspondence (including a few letters I have of her father's in return). Her father, Frank C. Lockwood, had sent her the manuscript of a book he had written about eighteenth-century English coffee houses. Mother admired his lack of adjectives and adverbs, she said (although in spite of her sensible advice, the book was never published). She would have made a good editor, I think. Possibly encouraged by being shown the manuscript, Mother described a story she was thinking of writing herself. Her mother picked up on the details: "I remember Mrs. Toll, her nice husband, her charming house, her pleasant garden. The dining room all filled with Delft. The red feathered bird that looked like a canary but wasn't and was imported from somewhere East o' Suez, also the sinister black cat that annoyed both Bitsy and me when we played in the garden. May the stories grow like Mr. Dinney's turnips."

MOTHER'S LETTERS

Her father was fulsome in more specific advice and encouragement:

> I hope you have roped and branded that short story. Put them down while they are fresh, under the first flush of the inspiration. I am sure you have a fine inspiration for a short story that some magazine will want. I think when you once get started you will write a good many such stories. So give expression to your moods and inspirations on the spot. Another thing: practice develops one wonderfully. As you write, you will find that you grow in ability to create plots too, and will be jotting them down all the time. Of course, no doubt, your chief qualities are stylistic and atmospheric and skill in characterization. But you will grow wonderfully in all qualities if you practice; and a little taste of success will whet your appetite.

Indeed Mother's skill in characterization is everywhere evident among the letters, be they from Europe or the ranch. Her father was probably right in thinking it would not have taken a lot to turn her material into fiction, especially when her subjects were other diplomats, or cowboys and ranch doings, or even the weather:

> Saturday, Mr. George Hanson who is the American minister to Abyssinia stopped over here a day en route to his post, and as the Consul General was away, Shiras and I had to entertain him. Shiras bought him bouillabaisse for luncheon, and we took him sight seeing in the afternoon. He is a big fat man and looks like Gov. Hunt. He lost his suitcase containing all his books on Abyssinia and official reports and instructions, so Shiras managed to locate it and have it sent on after him, and we lent him our Sherlock Holmes to read on the voyage instead and he seemed just as well pleased.

Her letters from the ranch were informative about ranch work, landscape and weather, and about people she and Shiras were involved with:

> Now I must tell you the sequel to the wild cow story. Mr. Smith came and we succeeded in loading them into his truck and they got safely

to his ranch, near Flagstaff. Last time Shiras was in town, the great excitement was the wild cows, who are now on their way home. They had gotten as far as the dairy in Williams, near the underpass, and apparently meant to return to their native cedar trees. Shiras says now he can sell them to somebody west of here, and keep on collecting $135 a pair forever.

The round-up went like clock-work, although Jim Bennet never would let Shiras get anybody to "help" him, but they got along fine. Shiras said several other outfits were shipping or using the pens for branding, the same day, and they all had quite a lot of men on horses. Somebody said there were more horses than cattle around, and Vic Watson [the buyer] said, "Oh, but you should have seen those Double A cattle come in." He was so impressed with Jim he offered him a job then and there, but Jim's goin' huntin'. We all miss him terribly. He's the best little man.

In a letter to her, Mother's father suggested two topics she might write about that he thought "not exactly within the realm of creative art, though highly worthy and likely to prove timely and popular." One was a biography of General Lejeune, for whom the Marine camp is named in North Carolina. Mother and his daughter Dena Lejeune had been college classmates and continued visiting each other; her father thought the two might collaborate in a book "now that the Marines are capturing the world." His second suggestion was a book about Mother's "ten years of experience and observation abroad as set forth in your letters to the family, supplemented by your vivid memory."

Mother would have been then in her midthirties. There is a typescript of a story of hers about a woman riding a bus, something Mother did a good deal in Washington; and later a cattle growers' magazine published a short story in a ranch setting, but the two "undertakings" her father mentioned I do not think ever were begun. It may sound deprecating or egotistical of me to sug-

MOTHER'S LETTERS

gest that "instead" Mother created literature out of letters home about the ranch and her children, but in all admiration, I think she did achieve that. I'd even say she partly invented us children as characters as she went along, our place in her letters substituting for the place that fiction might have taken had she not had children. Of course children are interesting to their parents and a fertile source of anecdotes, but I think that the four of us made her feel closer to her own mother and father, partly because of resemblances Mother saw between us and them, and possibly more so because we gave her a subject, better than any her father could come up with, to express her thoughts and observations.

As for myself, reading her now, I can see that how I saw her then getting along with my sister and brothers gave me the idea of what parents and children ought to mean to each other. Reading her letters confirms a sense I always had that she took comfort from Charly, Fifi, and Pancho, that she enjoyed playing with them, reading to them, admiring and being amused by them. I expect she did with me too, although I think I was a greater trial to her; her relationship to me did not look (at least to me) as relaxed as with the others. Also, because I was the eldest, I partly shared in taking care of the younger ones, sometimes to her exasperation: "She really has the worst disposition. She scolds Charly and Fifi from dawn to dark, and although they usually deserve it, her scoldings are much worse than the children's naughtiness."

Mother could be fierce in the defense of her children in a manner I expect I've copied. When we lived in Chevy Chase, Maryland, while Shiras was at the State Department, a policeman one day brought Charly home. The policeman had picked him up down the block, not because Charly had done anything wrong, but because he wanted Charly to point out some other children who had been up to something. I remember Mother on the front step saying things to that man I had not heard her say to anyone—how dare he take a child of hers without asking. She was wonderful, and I have not forgotten how, standing in the doorway, probably letting in flies, I felt her intense loyalty toward one of us. Of course she was critical as well as admiring of her children, but she seems to me seldom to have doubted us.

Charly was born in Bronxville, New York, and Felicia in Palo Alto, California, Mother traveling to the United States those two times from Marseilles. For Fifi's birth, we stayed with the Lockwoods, as my grandfather was at Stanford University on leave. Thus the Marseilles letters are full of these recent connections to her parents. She says to her father, writing of Charly, "Shiras and I both think he is mostly your boy as he is much more like you than like either of us. The other day I took him to get his hair cut which is a trial to him and he sat in the barber's chair with exactly your philosophical, benevolent look of enduring indignities patiently." Maybe that was why of all the children, Charly is the one who could most quickly make her happy. Mother loved baseball; she and Shiras went to games when we lived near Washington and New York, and she listened to games on the radio. Charly learned to quote batting averages right along with her. She wrote to her father after that return from California:

> Charly likes your picture that I have in my bedroom and Bitsy shows it to him often and asks him who it is and he says "Da" as though we were pretty stupid not to know that much ["Da" was what we called our grandfather]. Charly comes in my room every day and makes a bee-line for the picture of Da. There's a chair under it and he climbs up there and tries to reach the picture. One day I got it down and gave it to him to see what he wanted with it. He just wanted to kiss it, and he certainly made it smack.
>
> Your interest in the children always makes me so happy and even more so your understanding of them. I think you know them better than I do.

MOTHER'S LETTERS

Mother sketched us out:

> Charly is so nice and such fun these days. He really has quite a remarkable brain I think. He never forgets anything he sees or hears, so learning is absolutely no effort to him. He can't help it. Bitsy learns how to do things quicker, but he learns and understands ideas better I think. Charly is as happy and full of fun and has such a nice friendly nature that I see his main trouble is going to be that he's "a little too much the born favorite for my taste" as Capt. Smollett said to Jim Hawkins. He can always get away with much more mischief than any other ten children because he's so disarmingly sweet. He is also pretty sly and pulls the wool over one's eyes. Fifi is pretty nebulous still. She's very practical and clever at doing responsible little tasks, and to my surprise she has more imagination than either of the others. No, that's wrong, I mean more originality. Charly is the boy for imagination, everything he reads is real to him, but he's not very original.

Charly would have been two then, and not greatly changed from Mother's descriptions of him as newborn, when she wrote that "just at present he gives an impression of great dignity, strength of mind and force of character amounting almost to menace." Mother's frequent sardonic note makes her tenderness the more believable: "Tomorrow Charles will be a month old, and he has gained a pound and one oz. already and he often smiles and today he said 'Goo.' Bitsy was so excited—she came running to tell me 'Brother baby said "Goo," said Brother baby.' Isn't it funny how promptly little babies develop individuality? He's just as different from Bitsy as can be—serious and purposeful and composed, where she is gay and flighty and ethereal."

Whenever Mother mentions Charly, it is to describe moments of companionship:

> Charly is such good company for me. He is not irksome like Bitsy is sometimes, but very merry and interesting and full of thoughts.

MOTHER'S LETTERS

The book I have most enjoyed reading lately is Benjamin Franklin's Autobiography which for some reason I had never read before. What a lively, noticing mind he had and what good sense. Bitsy asked me what my book was about and I explained it was about a very sensible man who thought up new ways of doing things better. She said, "You mean really sensible, like Charly?"

Charly has become a regular little reading worm. He follows me around all day with one or another of his books, saying "yead, yead" and he knows Sambo and the nursery rhymes well enough to supply a word no matter where I stop. It's funny Bitsy never did like to be read to, but Charley likes it better than anything.

Charly talks allatime, allatime. He is such a great reader that he has lots of fun now when we take him places, because he recognizes so many things that he knows the names of from his picture books. In one book is a picture of a boat arriving in a harbor that we told him is the port of Marseilles. On our ride Sunday we went through the docks and Charly was heard to chant "Port of Marseilles." It was sort of startling to have him so right without thinking where he'd heard it.

Robin Hood and *The Desert House* are his great favorites. When it came to Robin Hood's death poor Charly got red in the face and burst into sobs and then had a violent fit of feigned coughing. He never would admit it was the story he was crying over. He said he just coughed. He drew a picture of the Heidi story which I enclose. The large brown mass is the cliffs, behind which are the goats. Apparently he was much impressed by the descriptions of the lovely sunsets, he drew my attention particularly to his spirited rendering of the colors in the sky. Did I tell you how Charly explained to Fifi what "minerals" are? We were playing "Animal, Vegetable, Mineral" and it was pretty confusing to Fifi that paper was veg. because it used to be growing in a tree, etc. So Charly clarified all by saying, "Look, Fifi. Minerals are what's not alive and never has been.". . . One day he chose a word which he said was neither animal, veg or mineral. We asked what category it did be-

53
MOTHER'S LETTERS

long to, and he said "General." The word was "Space," so I think he was pretty right.

With Bitsy at school every day and Fifi always taking a nap after luncheon, Charly and I have an hour every afternoon to enjoy ourselves together. Usually we read. We have just finished for the second time Howard Pyle's *Pepper and Salt* which you sent Charly some time ago, and now we are reading Charles Kingsley's *Greek Hero* book, which used to belong to me when I was little. Charly likes things pretty magic, with quite a lot of lions and tigers and dragons thrown in. He is fine to read to, because he is so wrapped up in the story and never interrupts with irrelevant questions, as Bitsy does. When we go for walks in the park we also play that game of yours of choosing the corners—it takes a long time to get home again, but it's very exciting.

This was in Montevideo, and she is right, the games Mother and Shiras played with us children seemed never to end. They also played with each other, as a game of hide-and-seek in which I was the hidden object (behind hats and gloves on the top shelf of the coat closet, among cleaning implements under the sink, or alongside the firewood under the stairway) and worried about what would happen if the one who was looking failed to find me. I stopped by the house recently when I was in Montevideo, on Calle Jorge Canning (it is now a clinic connected to the Italian hospital on the corner), and the receptionist invited me to step inside. The stairs and the short banister down the half flight into the living room are of polished wood, the banister with a rounded, spiral newel post at the end. For a child small enough, even that short run was worth sliding down. The height of excitement were the enactments of Jack the Giant Killer. Charly was Jack, armed with whatever sword, popgun, or other weapon he was carrying at the time. Mother, as Jack's mother, impoverished, pathetic, frantic that Jack would be eaten by the giant, was of course overcome with pride at his bravery. Shiras enacted the terrifying giant, somehow negotiating a slide down the

MOTHER'S LETTERS

banister to crash off the newel post as Charly cut down the beanstalk. In my return visit, the banister looked no worse for its clinical setting.

> I must tell you about another beautiful phrase of Charly's. I had a little party for Mrs. Morris [our Hartford grandmother, this would have taken place in Chevy Chase, when Charly was about eight] and the children came in to shake hands of course, and afterwards Charly told me that one lady at the party was "very enthusiastic" about him. Shiras thinks Charly gets his elegant vocabulary from you. Another time he came bursting in very happy and said, "Mother, this is a very fine opportunity for me. Mr. Tune invites me to play baseball." Usually Charly takes on considerable about cuts and bruises, so one day I was pleased and surprised when he exhibited a very skinned up leg without a single moan, indeed with modest pride. I asked him how on earth did he do that, and he said, "I slid into third base." . . . He frequently has "experiences" sometimes "interesting," sometimes "embarrassing" and occasionally "disagreeable." He was "rather annoyed" one day because I scolded him for not coming straight home from school. He'd gone to play with another little boy, because he was so "insistent."
>
> Charly and his friends have a Secret Club which has Secret Meetings in our basement store room to discuss Secret Plans. As the store room was an awful mess and the boys have cleaned it out admirably, I am the gainer so far, but as I have had to store two bushels of apples down there, I may be regretting my tenants a little later. Bitsy spied on the drawers of the Secret Desk and reported one drawer full of comic books and the other full of chewing gum, so I imagine the club meetings are given up to the most horrifying orgies.
>
> All the children have been sweet or funny or both lately. Charly goes to the movies as often as I'll let him, and learns many fascinating and useful accomplishments thereby, the latest being how to wear a monocle, which he does with incredible grace and nonchalance. Also

MOTHER'S LETTERS

how to shoot like a cowboy, as distinguished from a gun-man or a soldier. Charly is a pretty good air-plane spotter. He almost never misses on pictures of planes, and seems very confident about the real ones, although I am a complete dummy about it and never know if he's right or wrong.

When I hazard a guess that Mother could turn literary in her letter writing, especially on the subject of her children, I think that applies most strongly to her descriptions of Charly. She is admiring and bemused and feels close to him, but I wonder whether she does not also think of him as someone especially inviting to write "about," the way one would a character. One of her letters in fact does that; not long after the return to Marseilles from the summer in Palo Alto she composed for her father a playful fiction, in a Charly-character voice. Charly was two years old.

> Dear Lockwood,
> It was great to have a letter from you and to hear about all my relatives in America and about your books and travels. I am kept so busy with the many responsibilities of a man in my position that I have little time for letter writing. As you know I am practically the man of the family as my father has a consulate where he goes nearly every day and leaves me in charge, especially when Bitsy is at school. Of course when Bitsy is here, I am relieved of a great deal of the burden, because she knows absolutely everything and can reach to the tops of shelves and open doors and tie bows and button buttons. But there is a funny little object around here they call Felicia that takes a lot of my time and gets in the way continually. She is always on my mother's lap when I want to sit there and I am forever having to drop everything else just to go and take her thumb out of her mouth, a filthy habit she has acquired, I can't conceive how. I certainly do miss you, *mon vieux*, for what I need here is a man of my own age and interests such as yourself. These women don't seem to understand that I have my own life to lead and they are always trying to do things for

me, no matter how loudly I protest that I can do them myself. As if *I* would fall on the stairs if I didn't hold someone's hand! They treat me like a baby.

Aside from family responsibilities I also have a great deal of reading to do, my friend Cowboy (who accompanied me here from America) and Teddy Bear, to make comfortable and amuse, and my extensive building operations both indoors with blocks and outdoors in the sand pile to supervise and personally carry out as well. How I wish you were here to enter into partnership with me in these undertakings. I also have to help my mother a great deal as she always needs somebody to put scraps in the wastebasket for her, and bring her her shoes when she is dressing and throw away the weeds that she pulls out of the garden, and that keeps me hopping I assure you.

Let me thank you once more for your hospitality to me in America. Whenever you find a chance to return my visit, it will be the greatest pleasure to me to do the honors of Marseilles and take you for some walks and rides and show you our saloons. Your loving Charly.

There are appreciative descriptions of Felicia as well:

Felicia is such a good and inconspicuous baby that I always forget to write about her. She is five months old and weighs 14 lbs 12 oz. and cut her first tooth yesterday. Charly weighed 16 lbs 12 oz. at the same age but I'm not sure I'd want Felicia to imitate his proportions. She is so good and always delighted to be spoken to, but quite content alone. I no longer feed her at ten o'clock and it is such a relief . . . Her hair is going to be lovely—it is soft and fine and curly and a lovely red-gold color and I am going to let it grow so she can have curls around her shoulders. She is the jolliest, sweetest baby I ever saw. She is the only one I ever saw that could really amuse herself with toys at so early an age, but she is so contented with the big wooden beads Mother gave her, or her rattle or a "soft animal" as Bitsy calls them.

Felicia lived on the ranch several years after Charly and I had been sent away to school, Mother teaching her at home with the correspondence lessons of the Calvert School. In these years (from

MOTHER'S LETTERS

the mid-1940s), Fifi is less inconspicuous in the letters, having become Mother's primary companion when Shiras was not in the house. Mother describes Fifi's confirmation service in the Episcopal church in Williams:

> Fifi wore her new dress and taught Pancho how to behave in church. He was so good. He told me afterwards that Fifi told him he must be very quiet "just like in a museum." Pancho keeps saying "I can't believe it. Just think, Fifi is confirmed." There were only three little girls in the class, and it made the service seem so nice and intimate, with a small church and just the three of them. I told the bishop I thought it was so nice that he came just the same for three little souls as for a hundred, and he said he'd just driven all the way to Tuba City to confirm one. He added that the confirmation took place in the Presbyterian church and the Presbyterian minister had prepared the boy for confirmation. I thought this might interest your inter-church council, as I thought it was very nice. After the service coffee and doughnuts were served, and the pews shoved back and everyone greeted the three little brands snatched from the burning, and we chatted with Bishop Kinsolving and the rector, Mr. Frazier. Both are ever so nice. Now they have talked me into attending the Guild which meets Wednesday afternoons, and I am in a state, as I don't know at all what to do at a Guild. I hope we eat.

I have never been very sure what were our parents' religious feelings. When they left the ranch and lived in Tucson, my impression is that they participated fairly regularly in church events; my father taught English language classes sponsored by the Episcopal church to people from Mexico. In Williams we went to church, partly because it was an excuse, I thought, to get everyone cleaned up and into town, and do grocery shopping on the same trip. When we had come to Washington from South America, there had been a flurry of christenings, all four of us at once, but I remember no mention of church or religion before that. Religion was a sporadic experience in our family, it seemed to me, so that Fifi's thinking to tell Pancho to behave as though he were in a museum, and not the other way around, suggests to me that was true for all of us.

Felicia had an important moment in Mother's relationship to her parents when she stayed with my grandmother for a year, going to school in Tucson, after our grandfather had died. Our grandmother's health was not strong, and Mother visited her fairly often, but having Felicia with her made Mother feel, as she says, less far away from her own mother:

> It's so nice to think of you and Fifi being together down there. We miss Fifi awfully, but it seems to make you seem so much closer, somehow. Pancho is very funny. I think he misses Fifi more than he has ever missed anybody—you know he never minds when Shiras or I go away. He keeps saying "Mother, what do you think Fifi's doing now? Do you suppose she's running up and down stairs? Or taking a hot bath in a bath tub?" (Those were two of the chief treats Fifi was looking forward to.) I miss her too—I never can remember to set the table or fill the water bucket.

Felicia was a child to give Mother confidence, it seems to me. When Felicia started going to school at Verde Valley, Mother reports being "enchanted":

> There is a great air of excitement and intellectual adventures and enthusiasm there, and a very warm-hearted, friendly spirit, too. We were taken aside and asked what Fifi's chief problems were, and when we assured the teachers she didn't have any, they seemed a little disappointed, but they'll just have to put up with it.

After she had been there a while:

> We had such a happy visit with Fifi last Friday. She was looking so clean and neat and pretty, and in blooming health. She had just gotten her marks too, and had missed the Honor List by one point. This is judged on ability and enthusiasm in all fields, not just lessons. The point she missed by was Work Jobs, and her advisor was very comforting. He said, 'Fifi's work job is collecting and dumping trash, and

I'm not sure just how much ability and enthusiasm it's possible to show in trash-dumping.'

On one occasion with Pancho, Mother did not have to invent a narrative voice, she had her transcription of his own words to send her father:

I promised to send you a copy of Pancho's "record of everything" on his trip, so here goes. "It was the day we left and me and Nana played a game of cards and then Nana sewed up a hole in the knee of my pants, and then Mother came and I went to the bathroom while Mother called the taxi and we got in the taxi and drove to the bus station where we had luncheon and then weighed ourselves and as for me, I weighed 58 and Fifi the first time weighed 100, and then she gained 12 pounds I guess, because she weighed 112 when she did it after lunch. And then we waited for the bus, and we got in the bus, and we drove away.

We saw some poppies at Picacho and later we read a very exciting comic book and then we rode on and saw some gas tanks. And then we rode on a little way and came to Casa Grande where the bus stopped 10 minutes. And I went to the bathroom, and then got a drink of water and then got on the bus again. Then we wrote some more in this book that we are recording everything in (and then while the ten minutes still weren't up, I ate a Hershey bar, and soon, I think, we shall be going on).

We opened up my first sandwiches at Sacaton, and we traveled and traveled and traveled and traveled until we came to Chandler. And as for the present time I'm writing, there's not much more to record." The record continues until Wednesday, but that will give you an idea. Shiras thinks it is modern stream-of-consciousness writing at its best.

Pancho was born while we were in Washington, and like many last children in a family, was universally doted upon. Mother writes about him with a new joy, it seems to me, even though she was having to take care of him, in addition to the rest of us, without servants.

MOTHER'S LETTERS

Shiras had taken the other three of us to Dingleton. Mother makes her unexpectedly early trip to the hospital sound more of an adventure than the emergency I expect it was. Two months premature, I think Pancho remained in the hospital some days after Mother came home, but otherwise was a healthy infant.

> We had quite a thrilling time here lately. Shiras left July first with the children for Windsor, as the girl who was to take them got inducted into the Waves at the last minute. Thank goodness they left when they did, as it would be pretty awful to rush off to the hospital with no one to look out for them. Anyhow I stayed behind all alone in the house, and luckily was at market Friday morning with my neighbor Kitty Allen when I suddenly realized I'd better get to the hospital. Kitty was wonderful and even got all my groceries put away before she packed my bag and drove me to the hospital at noon, and the baby was born about seven. My doctor was perfectly wonderful and all went beautifully, in fact I had such an easy time of it, it doesn't seem quite real. Kitty telegraphed Shiras and he got back Saturday morning. I'm feeling perfectly wonderful, and really a little pleased not to have to wait two months longer. I'm taking care of the baby all by myself now, and trying to remember back seven years as to how to do it. Habit is so strong that I shall probably automatically pack the baby and his clothes and start off for an ocean voyage with him soon.
>
> I am strong now and enjoy doing things myself, it keeps me as busy as a switch engine. I feed the baby, I wash the baby, I wash his diapers, I concoct his bottles, I clean the house, I cook the meals, I wash the dishes, and I am also trying to make new curtains and bed spread for Bitsy's room. She has been moved out of her pretty room on the second floor to make room for Pancho, and I am trying to fix up the attic room for her so that she will not feel slighted. I've found some pretty bright red chintz with little old-fashioned sprigs on it, and I'm making ruffled curtains and a ditto spread with white ric-rac trim. The room is all white and needs some color. I think it will be sweet when done.

MOTHER'S LETTERS

My father collected us at the end of the summer while Grandmother and Aunt Grace were away for a few days.

> Shiras writes that he finds the children well but so terribly, terribly good that they will scarcely even laugh at his best jokes and antics any more. Apparently they have been living on a very high plane all summer. I can't say it worries me, as all the naughtiness they've saved up will pop out once they are at home again. Shiras' letter was very funny because at the beginning, having just cooked and served up his first dinner for the tots, he was rather pleased with himself and gave me the whole menu (delicious) in detail. At the end he says, "Now I must go and wash all the dishes from that dinner I cooked. I wish I hadn't cooked so much."

Mother always described Pancho as remarkable:

> Shiras and I think Pancho is the most delightful baby we've ever had. Bitsy was adorable, with enormous personality, but rather cross and bossy, probably because we were so afraid of spoiling her that we never picked her up to change her diapers or get up her bubbles, which would likely have improved her disposition. Charly and Fifi were as good as gold, but we were so occupied with Bitsy, and they with their nurse, that we never had any fun with them. But poor underprivileged Pancho has nobody but us to look after him, and we do enjoy it so. He is both good and lively, and wiggles and laughs if you just look at him.
>
> Talking of Pancho, he continues to amaze and to delight. He is the sweetest-tempered baby and the least trouble. He can sit up now, if we balance him carefully, a feat which neither Bitsy nor Charly accomplished till they were eight months old. He doesn't creep or wave bye-bye or talk yet, and I don't know why he should, except that he's so strong and looks so wide-awake and bright and intelligent that I keep expecting great things from him. He is so sweet in his corduroy pants. He has 3 teeth, and more coming, he eats vegetables and egg yolk and cereal, and you will be interested from the scientific point of

view to know that since he's been eating carrots, his hair has begun to curl. Fact. His eyes, I think, are going to stay blue.

I heard him laughing out loud when he was all by himself the other day and went to see what was wrong. He was playing with the blue dog Mother sent him, and just having a lovely time. He has learned to creep! He doesn't like to, and only travels for business reasons, when he wants to get his dog or his rattle, but he has a fine high-stepping action and he really does cover the ground.

Pancho is just perfectly wonderful. He tears around on all fours like a colt and stops and kicks up his heels with joy—once he gave such a bounce he nearly turned a somersault. He sings instead of talking, but he says "See-saw" and ee-a-oo for peek-a-boo and plays a dozen funny tricks. He is too beautiful for words and strong as a blacksmith. He and Crusoe are pretty suspicious of each other. Pancho likes Crusoe well enough but Crusoe is jealous of him and I have to hold Crusoe in my lap and put Pancho on the floor when they are together.

Pancho spent the most years of his life on the ranch of any of the children; Mother taught him from Calvert School lessons, and until he went to Verde Valley in seventh or eighth grade, Pancho had known only the ranch—from age two to twelve or so. His birth, combined with the move to the ranch, seem to me to have given Mother a new vitality; she reacted with a good deal of alacrity to the change from managing servants to building wood fires and carrying water buckets, and sometimes, I expect, felt a little desperation. But in my memory she was energetic, inventive, fun to be with. Her pleasure in Pancho combines with her pleasure in the ranch:

> Pancho asked Shiras to measure him today, and the result was 44″. Then Pancho asked Shiras how much he measured, and was told, 6 feet. Well, said Pancho, "I shall have to grow 2 feet and 4 inches be-

fore I am as tall as you." I had to take paper and pencil before I could figure it out.

Fifi has been entertaining Pancho lately by building the most adorable miniature ranch out under a tree in the pasture. She began with a log cabin shaped house, built of mud bricks, then she paved the yard with sandstone flagging and mud cement, then she built a fence and corals of Pancho's match sticks and string, with real swinging gates, and planted a sprig of juniper for a tree. Now she is modeling animals to go in the corrals. She has produced quite a recognizable horse, with a very stylish mane. Jim Bennet is just enchanted.

Pancho has been so entertaining lately. He has two new games. One is "playing perfesser" and the other is "playing judge." As a "perfesser" he puts a cushion from the sofa, with a fringe of crepe paper pinned to it, on his head, for he says he always sees pictures of perfessers with square hats, and teaches block-building. As judge, he wears no special costume, but sits on the flour bin, on top of the table, and solves mysteries, and very logically too. Yesterday, tired of hearing him jabber so much, I asked him why he talked such an awful lot. He said, "Well, its mostly questions, isn't it?" I said it certainly was, thinking in my innocence that I had him in a trap. "Well, I ask more questions than other people, because I want to find out about things. But answers I don't think I make any more than anybody else." So now I know why he talks so much.

Pancho had a friend named Two Eyes (from the fairy tale about One Eyes, Two Eyes and Three Eyes). He and Two Eyes would go off to the barn for picnics together, Mother packing a basket of peanut-butter-and-graham-cracker sandwiches. Pancho asked permission to eat Two Eyes's sandwiches if he didn't want them. There is a snapshot of the two setting out together, Pancho holding a little wicker basket in one hand, and extending the other to Two Eyes. Writing about Pancho meant Mother also wrote about the ranch, and I think many of her pleasantest associations there were with him:

> It started snowing again yesterday, and is snowing still, so everything is wonderfully pretty, and it must be 6–8" deep by now. Of course the skating has been sensational. Shiras and Fifi have wonderful fun, and Pancho shuffles about on his ski-skates, looking like a little cranberry on sticks, and from the expression on his face, he is swooping in graceful arcs and curves and flying over the ice, just like Shiras. He fell down pretty hard once, but he only said "Well, I don't think I cracked the ice, but it seems as though the ice cracked me pretty hard." Even Richard [Bargeman] and I got interested, and I took a brief whirl with Shiras' support, but Richard spent a whole afternoon at it, and got pretty good, said he could see where a man could have quite a lot of fun that way, with practice.
>
> Pancho paid his home a graceful compliment the other day, when Shiras took him to the drugstore in Williams for an ice cream. Pancho said it certainly was fine, such a fine thing to be in town, such a nice drug store. But, said he, it's nice at home too, in some ways. For instance, at home the tables and chairs, on the underneath sides, don't have any chewing gum.
>
> Pancho has finally won the consent of his mind to learn to swim. The first day Charley was to teach him, but he said to me, "Mother, won't you teach on me a little too?" So I tried teaching on him, but without success, and it needed Fifi to get anyplace with him. She is really wonderful with him.
>
> At breakfast the other morning, Pancho began laughing and chuckling so merrily. I asked him what it was about, and he said, "Well, I was just talking to myself, but isn't it all right if I do the laughing out loud?"
>
> We had a wonderful Christmas just the way Christmas should be. Pancho is just a dream of a six-year-old boy at Christmas time, and

MOTHER'S LETTERS

if you could have seen him sitting up in bed with his stocking toys, one in each hand, and another in his mouth blowing at it, you would have laughed. We have a lovely big tree, and the prettiest mistletoe and cedar berries and pinon cones I ever saw. I filled Fifi's flower box in front with cedar boughs, and covered the wire where the hop vine grows with a screen of pinon. We made one of our patented wreaths on a coat hanger and it is ever so pretty. My turkey was perfect. Shiras gave me some new sheets, which I was desperate for, and I gave him a pair of fleece-lined water proof boots which he says really do keep his feet warm at last. Talking of warm, we thank you over again every day for that fur blanket. It's such a comfort.

In summer, the rest of us were home:

Charly has been doing fine too. He has pulled weeds and raked and watered, scrubbed the kitchen floor and tightened my clothes lines. As Pancho never leaves his side for a moment, most of his spare time is put in playing baseball or card games with him. Bitsy has undertaken in addition to repaint the kitchen, which she has nearly accomplished, and it will look fine. All the woodwork is done now (every day there was a different cupboard door one couldn't open, but did by mistake, with you can imagine what results.) But you have lived through a painting job, I guess I will too. Next she is going to white wash the ceiling and walls. Charly is redecorating the linen cupboard—a hop vine around the edges this year, very pretty. Pancho has a great crush on Bitsy now, and I heard him telling her she was "nearly my best friend. If it weren't for Nana being my best friend, you would be." Once when his tooth ache was getting better we asked him how he felt, and he said, "the pain has been abstracted to the outer portions of my self."

I dearly love round-up time, its sort of festive and exciting, but cooking for six to eight people, with no Bitsy or Fifi to do all the hard work, leaves little time or strength for anything else. It seems spooky to be suddenly reduced to a family of two. Everybody and the cattle left for Ashfork Saturday, but Shiras has been commuting and came back Saturday and Sunday nights, and expects to be back tomorrow to stay, so Pancho and I are not alone very many nights. I had some hope of shutting up shop here and coming down to make a little visit with you while everyone was away, but I was just too tired to get ready for the trip, and besides there is some stock here that has to be fed and watered daily, which brings me to how proud I am of Pancho. Richard left him in charge of that job—one stray lamb, picked up with our cows, a dogie calf (Cactus Blossom) and a crippled heifer. Of course I thought that was pretty Utopian, and I would have to do it myself, but not at all, "that little boy, no bigger than he is," carries hay to his charges, opens gates, takes them to water, drives them back to their corrals and locks them up. He also feeds the cats and carries in fire wood, in addition to his regular duties. I told him he was worth one Fifi, two Charlys, and half-a-Bitsy.

There is a photograph of my parents and me posed in front of a white steam radiator. My mother and father are kneeling, and I, age two, stand between them. My father is dressed in a dark suit and tie, Mother in a dark wool dress I remember—it was green with a wide, soft, brown leather belt. Her left arm, the outside one, is behind her back. I too have on a wool dress, not quite as dark, smocked below the collar. The dark clothing against the up-and-down striations of the light radiator, and the white wall behind that, give the picture something of a Bauhaus effect. My parents appear young and pleased, and their eyes are toward the camera, Mother smiling a little more than she looks as if she thought she should. I am knock-kneed, my hands together, dourly staring past the camera with no expression at all. I have been told that Mother had snatched from my hands a ripped and dirty rubber ball and hid it behind her, and that an instant after the photographer snapped the picture, I broke into an appalling wail.

"As far as I can read her character from her handwriting, I think she has a sweet disposition but a nasty temper," Mother wrote home when I was three months old. I cannot help thinking I was

MOTHER'S LETTERS

a terrible interruption in my parents' lives (as a first child can be). By the time there were one or two others, Mother was referring to "the livestock I've been raising," but with me, she consistently sounds more anxious than not. It is a bit disquieting now to read about myself in these letters. I am moved by her joy—when she praises and brags about all of us I believe her that there were times she really was delighted in her children. I have felt the same often enough with my own. But her accounts of me raise other feelings as well—sorrow for giving her pain, and sometimes disappointment, anguish even, that she should sound so hostile, even though I realize with the passing of time, each of us grew a better friend to the other. What interests me most in her mentions of me are the glimpses some give of her more inner feelings, her doubts and insecurities as well as pleasures. I may, of course, be over-reading, as is easy to do when the subject is oneself; nevertheless her writing about the eldest of the "brats" seems to me to take a reader a little more deeply into her sense of herself.

My birth, in a school for midwives in Stuttgart, sounds to have been a catastrophe. I hear in her account—the way I did so many times—Mother straining to sound cheerful and hopeful, when I'd know she had given herself despairingly to some malady or other. When she was sick, doom settled on the household. "Nobody knows how I suffer," she'd say, only half meaning a joke.

The hospital she went to for my birth appears to have offered the best of pre-war German care—I was kept tightly swaddled, and Mother complained that she was not allowed a bath until I was five weeks old ("When I said I felt pretty dirty and uncomfortable, the nurse consolingly replied it could have been much worse in summer"). But she suffered acutely:

> I have been practically a nervous wreck ever since she was born, though the pride of the entire hospital staff, physically. I feel splendidly and get up twice a day for luncheon and dinner, and nothing

could be lovelier except when I get one of my fits of melancholia over nothing and nearly go crazy. However, they are getting fewer and as I get my strength back will go away I am sure. It's such fun being home again, and I am really as happy and have everything in the world to make me so. Shiras has been a saint all along, too patient and thoughtful and good for words. He used to come to see me three times a day in the hospital which is miles from anywhere.

Now her melancholy probably would be attributed to postpartum depression and addressed in counseling, or psychiatric care and medicine, but I don't suppose anything like that was suggested to her. My impression always was that Mother wanted to be cared for, to be taken care of, and I think my father did all he could, although I doubt it ever was enough. Knowing now a little of what that effort meant for all of us to keep Mother shored up when she was low makes me feel all the worse for causing so much misery for her so early.

She was able, nevertheless, to rally to a sardonic description of my appearance. At birth I had a lot of dark hair. She wrote: "She is short one eye brow but has lovely long eyelashes. Her nose is enormous, also her mouth and both just like Shiras' . . . She is really pretty when not crying." Ever grasping for a bright side: "The baby sleeps well and doesn't cry more than a third of the time, though she is indeed the big noise around here when she does cry."

Mother was twenty-four when I was born, and I enjoy "listening" to her discover her first infant:

> Johanna and Pauline told me one day they thought that the baby looked like her father and inherited her great intelligence from him, but to me she owes it that she is so dear and laughing and affectionate. Shiras and I are both a little dissatisfied with this clarification, but anyway you can see what a nice baby we must have, even if she does have a dumb mother and an unattractive father.

MOTHER'S LETTERS

On the fourteenth, to celebrate Bastille Day, the baby cut loose and began to walk alone. She could have done it weeks ago, but she's so timid about it. However that may be she just dropped our hands and began running around in circles. It was so exciting and she was just as proud and pleased as we were. Since then however I must confess she hasn't made much progress. Unless she's quite excited and intent on getting somewhere, and forgets herself, she won't walk without a hand to hold. She can though.

Her latest game is reading her beautiful book "Johnny Crow's Garden." She simply adores it. I hold it open in front of her and she turns the pages herself and when we come to a colored picture she pats it and laughs and looks up at me to be sure I don't miss it. Her favorite is the end paper, with the lovely giraffe eating roses. She always looks until she comes to that and then crows with delight.

It's too cold for Elizabeth to go out of doors so she plays in the house with us, but I think she gets fresh air enough as she always sleeps with her window open. Yesterday while I was taking a nap I heard her crying in bed and found she had kicked her covers off and was as cold as a stone. So I took her in my bed with me to get her warm and I have never seen her cunninger. She was so impressed by her unusual importance that she lay still as a mouse, only reaching her hand up to stroke my face every minute or so and saying "Ah-ah, mama, warm, warm."

It is good to know that such pleasing moments came along, for more often Mother complains of how "bad" I was. Surely there are elements in children that can make their parents afraid. In Columbus, when our children were in the half-naked diaper stage, I dreamed that one of them came crawling toward me on the floor, creep by creep, turning into a weazel. I don't know whether Mother feared she had a near monster on her hands, but at moments she may have. She tells of my scheming wrongdoing:

We have had a rather hectic week end changing maids. The new girl is very nice and though she has only been here one day, I am delighted with her so far. The hard thing was to accustom Elizabeth to her by easy stages, so I had to be there every minute yesterday, but it went very well. Elizabeth is a perfect rascal and she has given poor Anny a very false impression I fear. She was just as quiet and good and obedient as she could be all day long and acted like such a little angel with Anny that I fear me poor Anny has a shock coming when she gets back to normal again. Anyway her behavior was beautiful to see and almost fooled even her old mother.

Partly Mother blamed my bad temper on what she described as our two incompatible dispositions, but I wish she had said what she thought set me off on these rages:

I am fine though and we all are, except Bitsy who is enjoying a sore foot, and refuses to stir. The way she hurt her foot was that she had an awful tantrum and I put her in her crib till she got over it, and she threw herself about in such paroxysms of rage that she knocked her foot on the bed and apparently bruised a nerve—it's not sprained or broken but it hurts to walk on it. Poor Bitsy, she's such a darling when she's good, and really such a remarkable little person, if she didn't have such a dreadful disposition. The worst of it is, she is always good as gold when I'm away, and all these temper fits are just to celebrate my return. I wish I knew how to keep from upsetting her. I'm afraid it's just because my disposition is about as bad as her own.

Evidently her own mother must have come to my defense, prompting one of Mother's essay-like reflections:

You are a perfect grandmother and your remarks about Elizabeth being nicer than I let on, were just the right note. Because you have no idea how hard I have to struggle to suppress my enthusiasm about her. She really is lovely to look at—she is all over sort of honey colored from playing out of doors in her "birthday dress" and her hair is the same color. If anything, she is a little too overcharged with personality for such a small vessel. From the time she wakes up until she's asleep again, she's never at a loss for instructions to everybody. She is as good as gold though except when I'm around. It's my greatest sorrow—really it makes me miserable. She adores me and talks about me all the time and she weeps when I leave her and all that, but we just make each other wild if I try to stay with her. Perhaps I'm too severe with her and she expects a scolding whenever she sees me. Anyway I feel very pathetic peeping out from behind curtains to watch her and longing to be with her.

While I am puzzled to think what it was Mother found so difficult about me, I am moved by the revealing scene about herself—in any event, she is probably right that I appeared "bossy," in the manner of small children pretty set in their ways:

She likes to have everything that's done for her done properly and she's very particular. When I am taking care of her if I do something differently from Anny she fumes and complains and shows me how it should be done. She sleeps in Anny's room and one day I heard her in my room and my bathrobe was lying untidily in the bed. She was outraged and dragged it down and puffed and pulled it across the room all alone to the cupboard and so I hung it up on a hook, but she still wasn't pleased and finally I found I must hang it on a coat hanger and then all was well.

In addition to the complications of bearing a child and managing a household in a foreign country, Mother was faced with political complications in Germany that I am not sure she was prepared for. Some of the remarks she made to her parents strike me as simple-minded, and I am embarrassed by my own implication in her attitudes. I used to have to listen to my parents recount how, as soon as I could pull myself up on the bars of the crib, I saluted and said "Heil Hitler." Mother wrote of me: "Anny, the new maid, has taught her the goose step and she marches around the garden in the most Prussian fashion." When I was two: "The latest accomplishment is writing letters. She grasps her pencil firmly and puts her nose about an inch from the paper and mutters, 'Dear Papa, dear Mama, dear Anny, dear Milkman, dear Sandman, dear Hitler.'" To be sure, my mother and father were young, in their middle to late twenties; nevertheless, both were college-educated, and my father trained in foreign affairs. I can grant also that in the world at large between the world wars, prejudices against Jews and racial minorities were not unfashionable. Just the same, while I hardly think my parents were pro-Nazi, how can I think of myself goose-stepping and hailing Hitler?

Nevertheless, Mother had, as she says, "interesting times" to observe:

> Last week Shiras and I had a most interesting time. We went to a Nazi political rally, to hear Hitler speak. It was very interesting, though the reverse of what we'd expected. I'd always heard Hitler's followers were burning with enthusiasm for their cause, and that Adolf himself was one of the most fiery and persuasive orators of his day. On the contrary, I am forced to report that the audience reminded me of a Chautauqua crowd—having a nice quiet time and interested but not much moved. Hitler was a wash out. I'm enclosing a picture of that too. The meeting was in a little town about 40 miles from here and from there we went to see the castle of Liechtenstein which is marvelous at least from the outside, and the view and surroundings are too lovely for words, like a fairy story.

It may be that, writing to her parents, Mother did not want to worry them, that she was becoming fearful, and making jokes was a way to take courage:

> The great thing now is air protection, and it makes me pretty nervous, I can tell you, for how a French bombing plane is going to know I am an American I don't see. Perhaps if it flew low enough they could tell by my narrow feet. We went to a mass meeting night before last with 12,000 other people to hear about protective maneuvers. It seems that by fitting up a gas proof room in the house etc. it is possible to do away with a great deal of danger. Also everybody is obliged to clean

out their attics and leave them perfectly bare to catch fire bombs and during a raid one member of the household stays in the attic to put out fire bombs. I think Mr. Eitel (our landlord) would be the best for that. It gives me the perfect horrors to hear people talk as though such things were sure to happen and a matter of course.

It moves me to learn also that a nursemaid thought of a scheme, however hair-brained, to rescue me: "Johanna told me that if the Communists or the Nazis had a revolution, she was going to say the baby was hers and take it home to Oberalfinger and no harm would come to it and then Her and Frau Morris could escape better and not have to worry about the baby. This is the first I've heard of the revolution but at any rate we're all prepared."

As events in Germany developed into actual war, Mother's letters grow more somber, and by the time my parents lived in Marseilles and then in Montevideo, I know she worried a great deal about the war and friends in Germany, and was saying to her parents that she was too distressed to comment on international affairs at all. But in the early years, in Stuttgart, something in her remarks evidently offended her father, for once she wrote, "All right, I won't say anything more about Hitler."

Exactly what were my father's views, I realize I don't know. He spoke very little about himself, even if I'd ask, and Germany was a subject he seemed especially reluctant about. I do know that much of his time in Stuttgart was spent helping Jews leave the country. The politics of the family he grew up in were Republican and very conservative. He liked to say, only half jokingly, "Roosevelt, if you pardon the expression" before excoriating some event in that administration. The Lockwoods were Democrats and active in liberal causes, and Mother may sometimes have been embarrassed to report his Republicanism, as in this scene from 1943 with Felicia, who would have been six or seven: "She cornered Shiras in the garden and shaking a finger at him sternly demanded if he always voted for Roosevelt. It was a pretty tight spot for Shiras and before he could get an answer thought up, Fifi said, 'Well I always vote for Roosevelt or else for George Washington, but mostly for Roosevelt, because I guess George Washington is pretty dead by now. He's probly just a lot of old bones by now, probly.'" Shiras supported Senator Robert Taft for president, but when the Republican nomination went to Eisenhower, he gave up on the Republicans and gradually turned more liberal. During the Vietnam War, when he was living in Tucson, Shiras took part in antiwar marches.

On the return to Marseilles after Felicia's birth: "Bitsy is already speaking French again and is doing her best to run the entire household as usual." Much as she praised us, I never thought we children were quite good enough. She seldom referred to us, me least of all I think, without that edge of irony. Lest we think too well of ourselves, her phrase was, "You have a lot to be modest about." For all of Mother's efforts to reassure her parents that her life was safe and orderly, she continued cataloguing evil tales about her eldest:

> Bitsy's birthday, thank goodness, is over [I was three] and I have put the birthday child to bed and given her a handkerchief, and a dinkerwatter and said her prayers and kissed her and brought her dolly and so on. Next time she calls me for something I suppose I'll have to spank her, she is so above herself with all the birthday excitement. When I tell her she's a naughty girl she always giggles happily and says "Yes, Bitsy wewy naughty, but Mother love oo."
>
> She knows very well when she's naughty and she has a way she considers very subtle of rushing up to me and saying "Bitsy good girl. Bitsy kiss Mama" which always means she's been up to devilment of some kind. The other day she spilled some water on the table in the parlor and Shiras said she tried a new tack. She laughed in her best society manner and said, "Oh Shiras, looka dat. Looka what happened here. Gooness sakes."

MOTHER'S LETTERS

> Poor Bitsy has been almost as naughty and disagreeable since we got back as she was the first two or three weeks we were in Tucson. Sunday Shiras and I had planned to take her to the sea shore to play in the sand, a treat she especially likes. She was bad all morning and had a tantrum about getting ready to go, so we put her to bed instead and went off without her feeling perfectly awful and when we came home we were very austere and ashamed of her and ever since she has been lovely.

Second to being "good," my parents wanted their children to be polite, a virtue that apparently came to me more easily. But from accounts of what even Mother terms my excessive politeness, I wonder whether I was not honing good manners into further weapons:

> She is most polite and nearly every sentence is studded with pleases and thank yous. When she wants to play with Shiras she always says, "Shiras you like to play book now? Yes? All right. What book you like?" Shiras says he really feels it's very good of her to take such an interest in his polite amusement.

> We took her to call on the Gamons one day, and I reminded her in the taxi that she must shake hands with everyone. She is so conscientious about that, even including Shiras and me in her greeting, that I was not surprised when she obliged me to the letter, beginning with the butler.

> One night when we came in late from a party I went up to put her on her potty and she woke up very wide awake and said imperatively, "I must go see Shiras." I thought she had something on her mind so I took her down to see him and she said "Goodnight dear Shiras." Then she marched back up to bed and said to me "That was for polite."

There are any number of episodes Mother seems to be trying to turn into humorous anecdotes, but that in fact pained or annoyed her enough to place them in the "too overcharged with intelligence and personality for such a small vessel" category:

MOTHER'S LETTERS

> Bitsy is getting so foxy I can't keep up with her. Examples arise daily, but yesterday's will serve. She had one of her Christmas candies after luncheon and so far as I knew Charly did not. Later in the afternoon Bitsy came to Charly with her Lady Bountiful air and gave him a piece of candy. I asked Charly if he'd already had a piece and he said yes, but as I suspected him of saying yes just to be obliging, I said he could have it anyway, especially as Bitsy insisted he hadn't had any yet. No sooner had he popped it in his mouth than Bitsy said piteously, "Mother, if Charly has two pieces of candy today can't I too?" I said "But he didn't have any after luncheon you said so yourself." Bitsy said, "Don't bleeve me, Mother, bleeve Charly."

Admittedly, there were times when Mother seems amused by and appreciative of something I did, even when it might be turning a little too cleverly against her. The house in Marseilles had a wide cement staircase that curved into the downstairs hallway. I fell the whole length of it once, an event I remember well, and I remember especially not wanting to appear injured, always dreading being sent to bed: "Bitsy fell down stairs the other day but she didn't hurt herself. I don't know why, as she lit twice on the top of her head with both feet straight up in the air. She said afterwards when she had recovered from her scare, 'That's pretty quick to get down stairs, turning summer-saults.'"

In Bronxville, when Charly was born and my parents saw a good deal of my father's brother, Judson, Mother wrote to her mother:

> But the tea set was the big success with Bitsy. She treats it as though it were solid silver, and doesn't bang it around as she does her other toys. Every day when she's served us all our tea and bread and butter (Christmas cards on the silver plates are very tasty) she wraps it all up and puts it away again. She plays with it by the hour. One day last week Mary and Judson brought little Jay (15 months old and the cave man type) over to pay his first visit to Cousin Bitsy. Bitsy loved him and was so nice about bringing him her blocks and balls to play

with but when he grabbed one of her sacred tea cups she drew the line, and tried to take it away from him. But worse was to follow for Jay thought the nice shiny cup would be fine to throw at the wall and he sent it flying. Bitsy just stood and looked at him utterly speechless at such sacrilege and then she sort of moaned, in tones of more horror than I can convey, "Oh Jay!" We all simply exploded with mirth, it was the funniest event of 1934.

This scene is in a hotel in Montevideo, after a return from the United States:

Bitsy has been in great form the last few days. When she was staying in bed, Shiras and I used to sit with her when she had her supper, and it was always an occasion. She kept us laughing so hard we ached. Her reminiscent mood is one of her funniest, where she entertains Shiras with stories of "my grandfather and grandmother in America, not my grandmother Morris, no, my grandmother Lockwood, Nana I call her." The splendors of life at Nana's are almost unbelievable. "She makes the breakfast so pretty and she puts flowers in the toaster (I think this means the toaster and the bouquets of flowers side by side on the table, but I don't know). Da, he is so funny. Everyday he says such funny jokes and makes me laugh so much." Bitsy asked Shiras if she could go to school the next day and he said, "Well, I don't think so, it's such a bad day, raining and windy." Bitsy scornfully demanded "Is today tomorrow?" Shiras was crushed, but my turn was coming. I was sitting on the bed Bitsy was not in, and she said, "Mother, whose bed is that?" I said, "It's Shiras' bed." So she said, "Well what are you sitting on Shiras' bed for." I thought I would be too smart for her so I said, "What are you sitting on my bed for." Bitsy turned to Shiras and shook her head disgustedly and said, "Isn't Mother stupid, she doesn't know what she put me in this bed for!" Shiras calls this her Socratic method.

I must tell you of a conversation Shiras and Bitsy had lately, which he repeated to me. Bitsy asked Shiras which he liked better, Grandmother Morris or Nana. Shiras said it was pretty hard to say, but he guessed everyone liked his own mother best. Bitsy said, "But are you sure, Shiras? Grandmother Morris is a little severe." Shiras said yes, that was so, but still she was his mother and he liked her. Bitsy said "Well Shiras, I'm afraid I like Nana best. But you mustn't feel sad."

Bitsy was singing Old King Cole with a new verse the other day— "He called for his pipe and he called for his bowl and he called for his mistakers three." I was completely puzzled and asked what on earth mistakers were. Bitsy said, "You know, mistakers, those men he has to make mistakes for him." Shiras insists that is what she thinks ministers are, but I think that's almost too good.

When I lived with my family, it seemed to me I fit in less well than the rest. My parents and sister and brothers would sing cowboy and German drinking songs, and I cannot sing; they liked to play cards and board games but games bore me; they like parties, I am at a loss at parties. (Mother would get fed up and declare that for me, two was a crowd, and I dare say she still is right.) In her letters, Mother looks to be noting ways I do not somehow join in, sometimes even as an infant, for probably no larger motive than perversity: "I've been worrying because she doesn't talk more. Once in a while when I am about to despair of her ever learning she comes out with a whopping long word, perfectly pronounced. The other day she pointed to her sweater and said informingly and authoritatively, 'Pullover.'" But other instances sound to me to have less to do with a child's usual erratic pace of development than something more alien: "How long do you suppose it will be before she will take an interest in learning to read? She's nearly four already but I can't seem to interest her in book learning." Mother repeatedly said how she enjoyed reading to Charly, but I have to agree with her, I remember not liking to be read to: "Bitsy can rattle off nursery rhymes by the dozen, but she is no fun to tell stories to because she always interrupts to ask 'But what his mother did say?'

and when you're all through the thing falls perfectly flat because her only comment is 'why?.'"

Charly liked a Punch and Judy show we were taken to, and I did not. He evidently got the point and the right spirit, while I took it all too literally:

> Sunday we took the children out for a drive and we found a Punch and Judy show in a park and took them in to see it. Charly was charmed and sat perfectly still the whole time, only turning to Shiras or me every other second to say "Funny? Funny?" Bitsy however was terribly distressed and didn't like having them hit each other over the head. She told a little boy at school about how a robber came in the house and took some money and the policeman hit him over the head and the little boy told his mother that it happened at our house, so this morning people have been rushing up to me asking about the big burglary. All very complicated.

Mother does not actually say that I read mostly "pure trash," but she may have thought so. This was in Chevy Chase, when Nancy Drew was my idea of a perfect read:

> Talking of books, I must ask your help and advice about books for Bitsy. She loves to read to herself, but her tastes are very definite and pretty limited. She doesn't like sad books, and she doesn't like books about "the old days" (Robin Hood, King Arthur) and really only enjoys stories about little girls her own age. We've been reading "Tom Sawyer" aloud, and Charly and Fifi are spell bound, but Bitsy says it is just about nothing but naughty boys and she can't see what is so interesting about that. She likes the "Little Colonel" series, but they are pretty expensive, and the public libraries don't have them. Can you tell me of any second-hand dealer who might have them? Can you suggest any other stories she might enjoy that aren't pure trash? She liked "Juan and Juanita" better than any other story she ever read, so she can stand some excitement. Of course she has a good many Louisa M. Alcott books, and likes them, also "Rebecca of Sunnybrook Farm." I

am not much use to her, because at her age my taste was all for Scott and Cooper and blood and thunder in general.

When we all were home in the summers on the ranch, Mother sometimes wrote as though she enjoyed having us around:

> Bitsy and Charly have just made me a wonderful thing. I wanted a table to put under the trees where we ate a picnic dinner one time when the Reeds came. I wanted it big, so that when we have ten or twelve for a meal, we shouldn't be crowded. So Charly made a frame, of wood, strongly braced, and Bitsy chipped sandstone blocks for the top. Richard had brought a lot of thin slips from the quarries. It's really terrific—seats twelve easily and I'm sure there isn't another like it. My main rush about it is that Dorothy Lathrop Platt and her husband and children are taking a trip to the Canyon, the first part of August, and have promised to spend a day with us, so we shall be quite a big party.
>
> Saturday while they were away Bitsy and Pancho and I packed a lunch and went down to Corva in the jeep "algeritering" as I call it. We picked berries until I was *so* hot and tired I thought I'd drop and Bitsy was just beginning—said we didn't have half enough. Pancho said he wasn't tired, he just seemed to ache in every part of himself. Pretty soon we did stop, and Bitsy has been up to her ears in jelly ever since, and has so much she can't find jars for it all. We had such fun, and saw a big buck in the velvet, and came home by the new dam in the canyon.

Mother tells of that afternoon very close to the way that I remember it. Apart from my tendency to overdo a thing when I get going, the companionship so possible to enjoy with her comes through, a moment when she was not peeking at me from behind curtains. Indeed, as in letters written when I was going to school at Arizona State College in Flagstaff, she sounds to be writing of her friendship with me as a more and more sure thing. My going to Flagstaff, as I shall explain later, was in the face of considerable

MOTHER'S LETTERS

family opposition, and the culmination—reward, I might say—of years of my struggle against attending the schools I was sent to. I was never so happy as during my two years in Flagstaff, not since Montevideo at least, and Mother (for once) catches some of my happiness:

> Last Saturday was quite a gala day. We stopped in Flagstaff for a visit with Bitsy, on our way to Sedona, and found her just in 7th heaven. She had gotten the very job she wanted, lab assistant to Mr. Deaver, head of the Botany Dept. He is a sweet old thing, and Bitsy of course will soon have the Botany Dept. jumping through hoops for her. She was in that lovely state where she seems just to have walked down the golden stairs from heaven, and Shiras and I were *so* contented about her.
>
> My birthday was very nice and exciting. I invited Bitsy home to celebrate it with us, and she was such a joy. She and Pancho spent most of their time making a human skeleton out of horse and cow bones, to scare people on Halloween. I haven't seen it yet, but I can wait fine. [The construction hung from one of the rafters in the barn, and I must say was rather impressive.]

Mother tells of a weekend I came home, rode horseback, made mincemeat, and helped her and Shiras "clean two rooms in one day, and I've felt ten years younger ever since, not to have it hanging over me." College is supposed to be the time for breaking ties and going "away." For me it turned out the reverse, for I had been away every year since our coming to the Double A, and now, briefly, exactly as Mother says, felt I was "home." She mentions another of my visits, when she did not "think anybody ever revelled in a weekend at home so much." Mother had not realized how I had minded being away, she said, "but now I see she was just home-hungry."

It is hard to describe or even admit to my gratitude on coming upon these lines, not merely because I'd say Mother was right for once, but because here she appears to let down her guard a little

MOTHER'S LETTERS

from its usual relentless charm. That was what stopped me from reading on when Shiras gave me the letters in the first place. Mother had died mainly of emphysema, at only 63, after decades of a wracking cough from cigarettes, as awful a human sound as I can think of. I dreaded watching her play solitaire, bringing her cups of coffee, cigarettes and matches, emptying ashtrays. I dreaded most her taking to her bed when she gave up, and the sound of that gagging cough. My father too had smoked, but stopped after he left the ranch. Especially the last years on the ranch, both of them drank too much; Shiras stopped that as well, but Mother did not, and I expect drank more after she became ill. There was hardly anything I dreaded more than her unhappiness, recurrences I now see of those "fits of melancholia" that had fallen on her when I was born. The "charm" in these letters, therefore, comes through to me (quite possibly unfairly or mistakenly) sometimes as blatant denial of her truer feelings, and sometimes as near heroic defiance. There are also, thanks be, moments I recognize her sounding genuinely relaxed and nearly happy:

> The other day in Williams I got talking to the checker at the Safeway, who asked me where I lived, and when I said 'AA Ranch,' she said, 'Oh, I've heard about that ranch. Everybody knows about it. Why it's so well known, on account of what nice children you have out there.' Of course I told my little angels about the luscious compliment, and when I was giving them final admonitions about minding Mrs. Bargeman and being good while I was gone, Pancho said, 'Oh, we'll be good all right. We're so famous for it now, we have to.'" [She and Shiras were headed for a week with relatives in California, as I remember, and she reported the Safeway conversation happily.]

It was certainly a relief to her when we children were old enough to be left in the care of kindly neighbors (the Santa Fe stationmaster spent a weekend with us once), because Mother missed being around people more than anything. I don't think she realized, however, that she meant a good deal to the people who came and went about the ranch. The cowboy Jim Bennet, fond as she was of him, appears in her letters mainly for local color: "Jim is still with us, and such good company, at least between the things he says that he means to be funny, and the things he doesn't mean for funny but tickle us anyway, he is pretty entertaining. He told us last night he was raised in east Texas, where it was so swampy and unhealthy that 'it took two bull-frogs to live a month.'" But at least once he evidently surprised her when he came by the ranch on Mother's Day, on his way to visit his own mother in Flagstaff, full of his usual "I-could-of-told-'em-and-I-did-tell-'em" about how people did not pay enough attention to their mothers. Mother was feeling rebuked for not attending sufficiently to hers, who at the time was not well, but Jim Bennet was thinking of Mother as a mother herself, and had brought her a silk scarf.

Too many passages in the letters remind me of how sad and discontented she appeared much of the time, that however cheerful and well-observed her reporting, it comes to defy gloom:

> I've never enjoyed weather so much in my life. I must have written you about the fine rains we had last week. Now it's getting nice and warm with several un-windy days, and after the rain it's just perfect. The grass and flowers are growing faster than the cattle can eat them, and the weeds are growing faster than I can pull them. In the courtyard I pulled up everything except the lippia, if that's what I mean, and the filaree. I think the lippia will fill all the cracks between all the flagstones and nearly cover the yard if encouraged. It spreads such a lot. The filaree is so pretty in the mornings when the flowers open. Some of the trailers are a yard long this year. The two roses that survived are doing famously, the crimson rambler already has many buds. The Sweet William is in bloom already.

There is nothing factually untrue about the lovely scene—the weather could be wonderful, and with good rains the countryside look just as she describes it. Nevertheless, Mother probably would not have had occasion to praise so highly if drought, dust, bare ground, and dead flowers were not more often the rule, as with the roses that did *not* survive. Weather was everything at the ranch. If it did not rain by Fifi's birthday on the eleventh of August, the entire year could be knocked off as a disaster—no rain that came later would let grass grow enough to do the cattle good before shipping. Every year when it did not rain, and the wind blew, and you strained your eyes inventing clouds on the horizon, tales would go around about people who had gone mad looking for rain. Two extant rosebushes were indeed a triumph, of a higher order even than the six or eight zinnia stalks we carried buckets of water to night after night.

Obviously high on Mother's worry list was Shiras, who, for all his initial enthusiasm and ingenuity, grew more and more discouraged about the ranch, and the last year made himself fairly useless with his drinking. Nevertheless, it was always plain to me that he adored my mother, and she loved him in an admiring if exasperated sort of way. She'd say he was the only original thinker she had ever known, even though some of his thoughts were more than she always had patience for. I heard him say to her once, when he had come home from an overnight stay in town because of bad weather, that hospitable as his hostess had been, no one's company gave him the pleasure that Mother's did.

I was not always sure just how Mother took the clarity of his mind in combination with a nearly quirky absolutism, whether what sometimes struck me as hedging on eccentricity was what she meant by his originality. I seldom remember him angry, but a fit of my giggles could get me sent out of the room. He could not endure what he'd consider gossip, but saw folly everywhere, collected it almost, as when he reported how, at the end of a local cattle growers' meeting, it was decided to hold regular meetings on the last Friday of every month; several men got out their pocket calendars to make sure that every month had a last Friday. Dishonesty drew his

MOTHER'S LETTERS

rage. Shiras was called (only once) to jury duty in Flagstaff, on a case alleging fraud. During the process of selecting the jury, one of the lawyers, I suppose for the defense, asked jurors whether sometime surely each had not made mistakes in his checkbook. Shiras said that no he had not, and furthermore anyone who did he'd consider either very stupid or a crook. Shiras was bodily ejected from the courtroom and arrived home fairly shaken—his answer seemed to him so self-evident he was surprised anyone would ask the question.

One day Shiras took me and one or two of the other children with him to Flagstaff. What was the purpose of the trip, or why my mother did not go as well, I do not remember. The important event that afternoon was my father's going into a shop to buy Mother a dress. I had never known him to do such a thing. He sometimes went along when she shopped, and might give her jewelry, or scarves, or even a blouse, but an entire dress struck me as daring. It was an absolutely perfect dress: flared skirt and shirtwaist blouse in a linenlike, silky, oatmeal-colored material, exactly Mother's style. Shiras was conspiratorial with us, and firm as he consulted with the saleswoman; he did not hesitate about size. All of us were buoyant on the way home, and when we got home, Mother sure enough welcomed her gift with a joy to match my father's. She wore the dress often, and I never saw her in it but I was awed again by how much Shiras loved her, and she him in accepting the present so gladly.

When I was with him in Tucson after Mother died, Shiras became so grief-stricken I'd walk him around the block to forestall another fit of weeping. One afternoon I was at the card table answering notes when Shiras began fumbling about for his glasses. I jumped up, prepared to hunt. But he motioned me away, and from across the room, where he was holding onto the back of the winged chair, he said, "If your mother were here, she'd say 'Shiras, how *can* you be so stupid?'" It was her voice he wanted to hear.

School

There was a J. C. Penneys store in Williams where you shopped if you shopped anywhere. Mother and I went in one spring day, and up the stairs to women's clothing on the second floor. The stairs turned at a square landing, where, on a small table, was displayed a straw hat. We stopped as one, in awe before it. The straw was light and thin, the weave tight, the brim wide and undulating. Anyone in a Katherine Mansfield garden-party story could have worn it, but no one on a wind-driven Arizona ranch. Nevertheless, Mother and I longed happily for that hat. It was a fine moment. The hat came back to me a few years later when I was in graduate school at the University of Washington, getting ready for that event of universal anxiety, the general examinations. I dreamed that the exam took the form of a garden party, the faculty my guests, and I moving about grandly, making sure everyone enjoyed themselves, and wearing the Penneys straw hat. When the time came for the orals in a wakened state, I took the advice of that dream and treated the all-male gathering as though they had indeed been invited to my garden party, and I passed.

    For all the ingenuity put to verifying whether anyone learns anything or not, the matter of education seems to me to remain as mysterious as ever. Even after a lifetime of teaching and being taught, learning still strikes me as an erratic, elusive, although nonetheless actual phenomenon. Our son Andrew began training as a cyclist when he was twelve years old. "I'm going out riding," he'd say in the early afternoon, and be home for supper fifty or so miles later, along absolutely flat North Dakota roads, usually alone, the wind either behind or before him. His friends thought he was a crank. Teachers told him he was never going to get anywhere as long as all he did was ride his bicycle. He has got all over the world since with his bicycle, but it is hard for most people to make sense of a life dedicated to turning pedals mile after mile—the keeping on with whatever it is, unnoticed. I think I began to have an idea about such persistence during those years I despaired so of in boarding school. There was a pleasant room in an upper floor of one of the towers in the imitation-medieval classroom building. I went there at odd moments. One day a girl I liked found me and stayed a little while—we had English together in that room. Sitting by the windows at one of the long tables, you could see a good way over roofs and treetops. "You like to study," she said. It was an observation, there was no sneer in her voice, and I suspected she was right, although I had not yet myself had the thought. But I remember beginning to be conscious of the solace of slowly working something through.

Coupled with my own habitual seemingly mindless persistence, the garden-party approach to education is not a bad one, I think, if it does no more than lower the fevers schools induce. The rest is trying to look the least a fool. While studying and learning may be private, solitary pursuits, schools and classrooms are public places, and there, when I am a student, I know that a nearly biological tropism will gravitate me to exactly the wrong answer. The famous linguist and critic Leo Spitzer taught a course in French poetry one of the years I was at the University of Washington. I think I was the only student in the class majoring neither in a foreign language nor in comparative literature. The room was small, every chair full, and Spitzer and students talked in numerous languages and very loud. The day came for me to be the one Spitzer sprung on. I don't remember the initial question, but it was followed by several others I could not answer either, until at last he asked me: "Who is the greatest poet of the Middle Ages?" Relief almost exceeded my fright, I was so sure of the easy answer. "Chaucer," I said. "To the Anglo-Saxon mind, perhaps," Spitzer shot back, but had I heard of Dante?

As a student, I supposed that being shown to be stupid was what I was there for, but gradually I also came to observe how ill-equipped instructors were for appearing unknowing before students, or each other. Examinations must be the apotheosis of this shaming system, and it took little astuteness on my part by the time I attempted the Ph.D. to realize that while I might be the one under examination, it was not my brains the gathered professors were concerned about, but each other's. It would be up to me, like any alert party host, to save them from ridicule, to keep everybody happy; hence the usefulness of the hat dream. Ph.D. mythology is replete with stories of the event gone awry. A colleague had her examination on the first day of Lent. As the faculty, all men, gathered in the room, one, thinking of "Ash Wednesday," asked what poem of T. S. Eliot's was appropriate for the day. But my friend named another: "The Hollow Men," she said.

I had almost as automaton-like a reaction at the University of Montana, where the department decided that all of their six master's-level students should be smartened up with a battery of written and oral examinations. My *Thrall and Hibbard Handbook to Literature*, full of snappy definitions of literary terms, also lists in the back pages dates and critical events in the lives of authors. The excitement at Montana were courses in medieval and other literatures unmentioned at Flagstaff, and I had ignored American literature (still convinced, as Mother had observed, it was mostly boys' books). Nonetheless, in an examination gathering, I was asked what did I know about Roger Williams? Not a lot, I said, but (the chart in Thrall and Hibbard springing before my eyes) I did know that in sixteen-something, Roger Williams taught Milton Dutch. Nothing more was asked me on that occasion about American literature.

What rescued me from such predicaments, besides fear, was a certain agility in extracting the greatest effect out of the fewest grams of information I might have managed to store on any subject, a skill well-honed at the boarding school in New York State that my parents sent me to over every protest I could think of. I cannot suppose that either of them had any idea how much I did not want to go to school there. The two years of public school in Tucson (living with the Lockwood grandparents) had suited me fine, and I would have been very happy to finish high school there. But Mother and Shiras, as near as I can tell, had the idea that it was during high school that one learned the most, and therefore great pains should be taken that the best schooling be provided. To them, best meant boarding school. My views were otherwise. I was enamored of the ranch, of living in Arizona, and was beginning to feel a share of the lives of people there. I passionately resented having to abandon all that for what seemed to me a hothouse atmosphere in boarding school. The Tucson schools I think were pretty good—I was taking Spanish, Latin, geometry, and volleyball among the usual courses.

The worst that could be said for the boarding school was that it was snobbish and silly; the best, that there were teachers who took learning seriously. It was famous for its Communication Rules: you stood up in Chapel on Fridays to say whether you were "perfect," "imperfect," or "nearly perfect," according to whether you had talked to anyone during the week. The moments one was allowed to speak were few and far between. I could stand not being allowed to talk—silence solved many social problems, and the blue serge skirts and white middies we had to wear meant everyone looked about equally drab. There was a Latin teacher who scolded me roundly for having penciled English words between the lines of Caesar's Gallic wars, and when I said I was sorry, she said I was always saying I was sorry and should stop doing that, too.

SCHOOL

The grounds of the school were lovely, with huge beeches and other shade trees, the food was good, the rooms comfortable enough. There were girls I liked, and two or three teachers I admired. It was the way of life that the school represented I rejected as well as the thought of the high fees my parents were paying. Missionaries came for Sunday evening chapel to tell us of good works to be done, but probably not, I gathered, by us. As near as I could tell, we would be marrying rich men, and doing good deeds by check. I heard no one mention earning a living, entering a profession, developing talents. The art teacher was highly serious about our paintings and sculptures—she put some shadows next to trees I was trying to paint in such a way that the shadows actually lay on the ground, magic to me—but I do not remember that talented girls were being told how they might themselves become artists. At the dinner table once I was going on about the ranch, the cowboys and woodcutters and quarry people. The girl sitting across from me—she was wearing a purple tie that meant she was on the Student Council, and she was president of nearly everything in sight—asked me did I really associate with people like that? I suppose her question helped me to realize that I did.

About half the girls went on to four-year private colleges, and the rest who were not marrying right away, to junior colleges, with graduation to the Junior League. Aspirations did not appear to reach elsewhere. So just at the time when, looking at the ranch and the rest of Arizona, I thought I had found the kind of life I wanted to lead, the school represented just as emphatically what I wanted no part of. I can only suppose that my parents did not become conscious of my desire, and try as I might, apparently I failed to give them a hint of it. There was worse to come. After boarding school, my parents, and then Grandmother Morris as well, decided I should go to Wellesley. Grandmother would pay the fees. I cannot convey my rage and despair. Of course this was a fine opportunity, as Charly had said of his invitation from the baseball coach, and I might well have profited from it were I going from school in Tucson. But all I could see was my own life, whatever that might become, held off again. To keep the family peace, I said I would go one year, and I did.

Not returning to Wellesley after the conciliatory freshman year (1950–51) cut me off from my grandmother's munificence, and there was little coming from my parents either. I had supposed I'd be at the university in Tucson, until Mother suggested Flagstaff. I don't know what made her propose that—pique perhaps, though I hope not. I remember first my surprise, then absolute delight, for although I had not thought of the idea myself, once she did, I felt the excitement of new adventure. She could not have had a better thought; the fact that it was hers may have helped her to imagine my desires a little differently. At any rate, it moves me now to read her pleasure in settling me in to that tiny campus where we'd joke about the college slogan, "It's great to be a lumberjack."

> We took Bitsy over to Flagstaff on Monday, and I was so surprised and delighted by all that I found there, that I really feel Bitsy will have a wonderful year. I remembered the run-down Normal School Sister and I went to, and found instead a real college, with beautiful buildings, a great impression of friendliness and enthusiasm. Bitsy's room is in a new dormitory, which is just de luxe, with ironing boards, hair dryers, Bendix washing machines etc.

The dormitory may have been new since Mother's Normal School days, but I hardly thought it luxurious—I don't know where she saw hair dryers, and the one slosh-around washer had to be kicked severely before it would start. The building was handsome, though, of hand-cut sandstone. A dubiously endearing feature was the fire escape, a pole at each end of the single long hall. At fire drills, you stood on the edge of the window sill, reached for the pole, and slid down, received at the bottom by residents of the boys' dorm. I was elected fire chief for my end of the hall. One week-

SCHOOL

end there was a high school journalism conference on campus, with extra girls in the dorms. At two in the morning the fire alarm went off, and with that dreadnought executive ability Mother attributes to me, I had all the girls in my watch out of bed and down the pole in record time—and several moments before anyone told us it had been a false alarm. It seems one of the journalist students had come in after hours, shinnied up the pole, and unbeknownst to her friend who opened a window to let her in, set off the alarm. I think I was in worse repute than she.

My father paid for books and fees, I worked in the biology department at fifty cents an hour for board and room (the working hours adjusted to correspond exactly to each month's housing bill), and baby-sat for pocket money. I finished three years in two, with intervening summer sessions, and was exhausted by the end, but exhilarated that finally I had been the main one in charge of myself. I still rather marvel that my parents acquiesced to it all.

Mother was right about my pleasure at Flagstaff in securing the job with Mr. Deaver, the botanist (thanks to the student he had previously hired not showing up). Mr. Deaver had happened to come out to the ranch that summer to look at some dying juniper trees whose malady my father was hoping to encourage as a way of weeding out junipers. Mr. Deaver thus being my single acquaintance, he was the first I went to, qualified only with the very rudimentary skills of a semester's high school typing class. More than a job, this was an experience for the first time unconnected to my parents, and it turned out also to tighten my connections to Northern Arizona. I typed multiple-choice botany tests on mimeograph stencils and ran them off on inky drums in a basement closet. But more enterprising was my work in the herbarium, where Mr. Deaver was accumulating a distinguished collection of plant specimens, from above the timberline on the San Francisco Peaks to the desert around Sedona, with the rich foliage of Oak Creek Canyon in between.

SCHOOL

In the herbarium I'd lay out plants on thick gray blotters, lifting blocks on and off, and changing the blotters every day until the plants dried. I typed identifying labels, arranged the dried plants on sheets—attempting pleasing designs, for which the lab assistants teased me—and filed the sheets in metal cabinets. The janitor, who had been gassed in the First World War and sometimes fell down the stairs or through glass doors, liked to talk to students working about the place. He would lean on a mop against a door jam and comment on my sorting weeds. Mr. Deaver was patient with my typing, which must have been very bad, and he was generous in inviting me along on field trips when there was room in the car. One spring the Little Colorado River flooded, a rare event for a dry river bed. Several of us persuaded Mr. Deaver to drive out to see it. There was not a plant in sight, but we took each other's pictures on a rock in the midst of tumbling thick brown water—the river, we heard, was nearly dry again the next day. For me, Flagstaff mainly was this fifty-cents-an-hour job.

I thought Flagstaff the most beautiful place I had ever seen—pine trees, flowers in the yards, aspen and wild flowers and open meadows on the San Francisco Peaks. Compared to the more arid topography of the ranch among juniper trees, sandstone quarries, and limestone gullies, Flagstaff appeared an oasis of moist, nearly lush mountain terrain, and a luxurious center of culture. I have no trouble believing that the Kachina gods of the Hopi Indians, as it is said, live where the tops of the mountains have hollowed out a bowl. The very air inspired joy. As a girl, my mother had spent summers there while her father ran the university's summer school. She and her younger sister went for horseback rides and picnics and generally amused themselves during those idyllic summers. Mother liked to tell how her father admired the stone house at the head of the valley north of town, and as they rode their horses past it once had said that was where he'd like to spend his last days. He probably would, Mother told him, for the building was the county poor farm.

Arizona State College at Flagstaff, to give the place the title it had in the early 1950s, had not long emerged from being the Normal School of my mother's day. The campus consisted of some six buildings, some of sandstone, around a circular drive, a few World War II surplus Quonset huts, and stone cottages for married students, mostly veterans and their families. The central classroom building was of hand-cut sandstone, its thick walls, turrets, and castellated trimmings giving that air that some early academic buildings in the west have of benign fortification. Beyond the cottages up a slope was a cemetery, and on its edge an observatory was being constructed by the Air Force. On Sunday evenings my friend Janice and I liked to climb the scaffolding and eat our cafeteria box supper on the platform where the dome was to be set. We could see a long way from up there, to the rose college buildings next to Highway 66, the lumberyard across the road with its cluster of workers' shacks, and the town and mountains beyond. (Flagstaff still held a reputation for clear air that had attracted the founders of its Lowell Observatory.)

Yet for all its bucolic setting, not even Flagstaff could preserve me from the ridiculous. Shakespeare class one summer met in the afternoon just after lunch, when I was not the most alert of students. We sat rather crowded in a second-floor classroom, in wooden armchair desks, arranged in rows that went sideways across the room. The view out any window always was lovely, of trees and hills and mountains. Nevertheless, it got hot, and I could become hopelessly sleepy. My books were stacked on the arm of the chair, my elbow on the top book, my hand holding my head, and I, one afternoon, asleep. The voice of the woman who taught the course startled me awake—something disparaging was being said about people who fell asleep in class. Then the books dropped off the chair, and so did I, picking up chair and books and myself among the feet and legs of other students.

Whatever is meant by "learning"—the acquisition of information, the better understanding of its implication, a passage of sorts from innocence to experience—such discovery itself can appear ludicrous. The more important the discovery to myself, I've found, the sillier I can think I look. So it was again in this Shakespeare class. One day a paper for the course was returned to me with a note saying that if I included material out of a book I should "use quotation marks." Puzzled, I showed the professor that I had indented lines from the play, and was not that how quotations were indicated? She was referring to longer passages, she said, and mentioned a book by someone named Van Doren. The conversation seemed at cross purposes, but I was curious, so I went to the library and found a book by the author Mark Van Doren, who I could see wrote essays on the plays of Shakespeare. Not only that, I was standing before entire shelves of books *about* Shakespeare. I had not known that people wrote books about other books, and still can feel the warmth of embarrassment at that discovery.

Academically, the two years at Flagstaff turned out more muddled than not. I whittled soap carvings for an art course from the back row of an economics class. There were three male students and me taking taxonomy; the instructor could not give everyone an A in the course, he explained, so because I was the only girl, I'd be the one with a B. When I wasn't in the science department, I sought out the library, but getting into the stacks required a special card, which I almost never had with me. I'd slip behind the counter when I hoped no one was looking, resulting in the librarian's more than once chasing me up and down the aisles. One night I fell asleep at a table in the deepest recesses of the top level, until discovered by the fairly disgruntled librarian who had locked up but returned for something she forgot.

I have from Flagstaff a little gold ax, an It's-great-to-be-a-

SCHOOL

Lumberjack award, though I cannot claim much there in the way of academic distinction. However, Flagstaff suggested the direction that my pleasure in school might take. I began thinking I'd major in history—it was interesting, and because history was hard for me and I didn't understand it very well, I supposed it worthwhile. Also, the professors on the faculty at Flagstaff who appeared to me the most learned were historians—elegant Professor Tinsley, from one of the Carolinas, who explained the great moments of English history with scenes from English novels. Then the obvious occurred to me, that I might major in English and for rest of my life read books. I shan't forget the simplicity of the solution, and relief at realizing I could do that. Instead of putting off, after botany, or history, or gluing plants, the authors I cared more and more about, there was every chance those books could become the way to my livelihood.

My beginning in this new livelihood, a job teaching tenth grade English and biology at the high school in Prescott, Arizona, was not auspicious: I was fired. The high school campus was pleasantly set in what had been a swamp on the edge of town, an early example of urban renewal I expect—three one-story buildings around a quadrangle, grass in the middle. I lived at the top of the hill in Prescott, on Gurley Street, in a cottage behind the landlord's house, from where I could just barely see the San Francisco Peaks at Flagstaff. Typical of first-year teachers, I fought off rubber-band attacks from the back rows. I don't think I did particularly badly, and on the whole, enjoyed the year.

Nevertheless, some time in February, the principal called me to his office to tell me I would not be hired the following year. He said I had "a bad reputation," but would not say for what. I called on the superintendent some days later, with what I hoped was an air of respectful humility. I had settled on teaching as an occupation to earn my living, I explained, and if he thought me unsuited to teaching, would he tell me how I fell short? What he said was that as far as teaching English went, I was as good as anyone in town. And I still don't know. (If by "bad reputation" he meant sex, I saw no friends male or female that year, as everyone from college at Flagstaff was teaching or in graduate school. And anyway, unacceptable sexual behavior hardly strikes me as an unmentionable subject for an administrator firing a teacher.) As a practical matter, not being able to return to Prescott may have been a good thing by precipitating me to graduate studies in Montana.

Strangely, now that I think of it, no one at Flagstaff had suggested graduate school earlier, but hearing of my demise in Prescott, someone in the English department sent me a notice of assistantships available at the University of Montana in Missoula. I knew nothing of what graduate studies might entail, but admiring my Aunt Mary Margaret who had an M.A. in English, and having no other employment, I thought there was everything to gain in applying. The family was dubious—Pancho looked up Missoula in the encyclopedia to learn that after the presidential election of November eighteen-hundred-something, results had not reached Missoula until the following spring.

Still, away I went, and in two nights and days by Continental Trailways arrived midafternoon, suitcase in hand, at the doorway of a classroom in which Walter Brown, director of Freshman Composition, was instructing new teaching recruits. My arrival—perhaps I was more disheveled that I realized—put a stop to the proceedings, and I was taken, something like bounty I felt, to the house of Leslie Fiedler, then chairman of the English Department. I knew nothing of him as critic (this was the fall of 1954, when he had published a volume with the scabrous essay about "the Montana Face" and was giving lectures that became *Love and Death In the American Novel*). I had never read the novels of Walter Van Tilburg Clark, who I think also was at the house when the Composition contingent arrived. Fiedler offered a long list of drinks, ending with tea. I warmly asked for tea. Mrs. Fiedler made a pot, which restored me wonderfully; later I learned that at the Fiedlers no one ever had asked for tea.

For all my family's world travel, Missoula was a spot I was the first to get to. It looked to me not more beautiful, but a good deal more lush than Flagstaff—grassier lawns, more flowers blooming, little rivulets flowing out of mountainsides into the canyons. It excited me to be right in among the mountains. But not so a student in the composition class I taught. He was from Sidney, at the eastern edge of the state, and told me one day how homesick he felt. But Missoula was so beautiful with all the hills and mountains about, I said, trying to cheer him a little. That was the trouble. "When I stand on my back porch at home," he said, "I can look out and see something." Now that I live in his terrain, I know what he means. You "see" to the horizon in every direction. I also remember thinking Missoula more up-to-date than northern Arizona, where along Highway 66 even in the mid-1950s you could count fewer Arizona license plates than ones from California or New York. Mother wrapped her bread in dampened diapers, plastic bags not having appeared yet. The Missoula Mercantile sold plastic bags, and I sent her a package, feeling advanced and modern.

Thrall and Hibbard notwithstanding, I expect I left the University of Montana with the academic experience most M.A. students start with, given that at Flagstaff, Chaucer, Milton, Blake, and the eighteenth century all were unclaimed territories. Fiedler, delivering freshman humanities lectures on Samuel Richardson's novels, was a genius with young Montana students, I thought, though I wondered whether they'd find *Pamela* or *Clarissa* up to his descriptions of those books. His lectures sent me to the large subliterature of gothic novels, closet drama, and the weepy fiction of the eighteenth century, and his sometimes sardonic remarks could feel encouraging. I was sitting near him in the auditorium one morning waiting for another one of the faculty to begin a humanities lecture, when the person next to me asked what was I reading. Fiedler interjected, "Elizabeth reads only strange and depraved literatures." In a course on the epic he assigned me to report on Byron's "Manfred," the verse drama replete with lengthy declamations from cliff ledges and ending with the hero's line I thought particularly silly: "Old man, 'tis not so difficult a thing to die." When I finished talking to the dozen students in armchairs before me, Fiedler said that mine was the clearest and least sympathetic reading of Manfred he had ever heard.

At Missoula not only was I shown ways to begin reading and thinking about literature, but I developed strong friendships as well. One of these was with the Freeman family, who would insist I stay for supper, when, tired at the end of the week and not having much left in my own larder, I'd stop by late on Friday afternoons. Edmund Freeman's Blake course at eight in the morning made it easy to confuse his visionary goodness with Blake's. Mary Freeman wove on a loom in an upstairs bedroom—mats, pillow covers, and eventually an enormous rag carpet in fading shades of red, made of discarded hotel draperies and covering the entire front lawn. It was for their son's house, in King Of Prussia, Pennsylvania, and they took it to him my first summer in Missoula. I lived in their house for the month, caring for Mrs. Freeman's mother, Mrs. Bizelle, who had lived in Kansas City and subscribed to two Kansas City newspapers. Mrs. Bizelle could, and invariably did, tell you what was going on in Kansas City. I also tended Mr. Freeman's vegetable garden, picked dishpans full of strawberries for jam, and otherwise had the run of the wonderful house, cool and light and shaded.

The Freemans made the same trip the next year, and again I tended to Mrs. Bizelle and the garden. A couple of weeks into my stay, I lay one afternoon on the living room couch reading the eighteenth-century gothic horror novel known as *Monk Lewis*—death and bleeding paintings and young girls chased through corridors and alleyways. Hearing Mrs. Bizelle stirring upstairs, I roused myself to take her a glass of orange juice. She was sitting in her wicker chair, the letter she was writing on her lap, and she was dead. The doctor, on the telephone, asked me how did I know she was dead, but when he arrived, agreed she was. Together—he her shoulders, and I her legs—we lifted her onto the bed. Mrs. Bizelle was cold, just as dead people are said to be ("key-cold" in *King Lear*). When I called them, the Freemans told me to arrange for her body to be sent to the family home in Missouri where they would go for burial.

Then I called undertakers. The two men who arrived from the funeral parlor were unable to get a stretcher up the narrow staircase. They were obliged to drape Mrs. Bizelle between them —she could not have weighed ninety pounds—and when they started down the stairs, one said to me over his shoulder, "These old houses just aren't made to carry people out of." Coffin shopping was no more edifying. I was shown the $1,200 copper-covered model, then spotted a gray casket for $200. But it would not do, the man said, it was a male casket. I asked what was a male casket. Female caskets, it turns out, have a side panel that hinges down, and extra lace on the pillow. I said I would buy the male model, in spite of the undertaker's protests that the Freeman's status in the community might thereby be diminished.

The English Department at the University of Montana offers no Ph.D., a restraint for which I admire them, but they have a good "feeder" relationship to the University of Washington in Seattle. Thus, following the encouragement of Leslie Fiedler and others that I continue graduate work there, and with the help of their recommendations, I applied and was accepted.

Seattle, too, had its gothic event in the collapse of a sewer main not two doors from me, apparently giving way in an underground fault, and causing a large tree, along with a section of boulevard, to disappear into a crater. The street was cordoned off and for weeks

I rode my bicycle through a police blockade to reach the garage-turned-apartment where I lived behind a hedge of deadly nightshade. Ice cream trucks were parked at the barricade for the benefit of sightseers, and I overheard a woman in a grocery store say to her fractious youngster, "If you don't behave, I won't take you to see the hole."

At the University of Washington it was generally understood that to ensure good recommendations for a college or university teaching appointment, male graduate students needed a B average; women with Bs vanished into community colleges, book sales, or marriage. The revival of the feminist movement was still several years away. As women students, I think all of us agreed, we received equal treatment with the men as long as we were as able as the best of the men, but the time had not yet come for women to be "average." On another point where I think gender made a difference I can speak only for myself: I had an extraordinarily good time in Seattle, in face of the growing vogue of hating graduate school. The men were anxious about grades; they were bent on pursuing a prestigious career. Several were married, their wives working; a few had children. All these circumstances exerted personal and professional pressures. I, on the other hand, felt no pressure from anyone.

Hardly anyone I knew understood what I was doing or supposed it would last very long, and for that matter I was loath to admit I thought so either. Each quarter was a fresh surprise when passing grades were mailed me, and so I'd register again, hoping to beat the odds once more. It surprises me when I think of it now that Mother and Shiras took little interest. I had all but lied. A degree from the University of Montana, I told them, would help me get a better high school teaching job. But that excuse hardly held for the effort of a Ph.D., so this time I pointed out that the assistantship paid $200 more than I earned at Montana, as though I were improving myself in a line of work. (By the time Felicia and Pancho earned their graduate degrees, and Charly went to law school, our parents seem to have been more used to the idea of postcollege education.)

At any rate, as no one expected much of anything from my venture, I was as free as one can be to enjoy the classes, the company of other students, the city of Seattle, and my garage behind the deadly nightshade. In one sense, of course, this almost holiday feeling probably came from low expectations of myself—I worked like fury and had no intention of "failing," but on the other hand truly was amazed that my head floated above water. Economically I also had no intention of not being independent. I could live comfortably on the assistantship, and if the whole venture really did collapse, there was always high school teaching to fall back on. These were days of teacher shortages and fairly good pay; with an M.A., I'd be eligible for an even better job than before, as long as I did not apply in Prescott.

Which is not to say I did not feel apprehensive. Other students I could see were far more knowledgeable than I about almost anything, but I may have had a small advantage for a sense of play. In a criticism class we were given a sheet of poems unidentified by authors or titles and asked to evaluate them, the school known as New Criticism being current at the time. One of the poems I recognized in the exercise was by Ella Wheeler Wilcox, the popular sentimental poet of the early twentieth century whom I had come upon in my pursuit of the strange and depraved. A student who had not spotted her hand presented an elaborately learned analysis to show how in every respect her poem conformed to the requirements of New Criticism, and therefore was a very fine poem. I confess to an evil pleasure in harassing him—the more earnest his elaborations, the more I twitted the poem.

The move to Seattle convinced me more than ever how much I cared for studying, for classrooms, teaching, the company of other students, nearly everything about the academic setting, as well as literature. Joy came partly from surprise. So much of education had meant fooling teachers that I had acquired some skill in inventing answers to questions I did not wholly understand, but it was not a skill good for much else. A difference that came about in Seattle was that instructors were showing an interest in what students themselves might be able to do, and they were encouraging us to continue improving in what we already began to do well. Some of what I did not know did not any longer seem to matter. For a course on Milton's poetry taught by Arnold Stein, then completing his second book on Milton, I wrote a paper on imagery in *Paradise Regained*—feet and walking are mentioned a lot, yet I had read that that long poem was thought remarkable for having almost no imagery. Stein talked to me in his office about the paper in a friendly way; he found it interesting, he said, even though it was not a paper he would have written himself.

This degree of respect at first caught me off guard when I began to encounter it after so many less-encouraging years in classrooms. It also took me back to the days at the Crandon Institute in Montevideo where, I had always thought, there existed a school that actually succeeded in being whatever it was school was supposed to be. There the two Payton sisters (Miss Payton and the younger Miss Maggie Payton) who taught in the lower grades were nothing if not strict—many a late afternoon I stayed to be drilled in multiplication tables. I had missed first grade entirely (thanks to an intestinal disorder common enough among Northern Europeans but apparently unknown among the southern immigrant descendants and noted by a doctor in a footnote to a medical journal article just in time to rescue me). Mother had sat on the edge of the hospital bed with the reader—its title was *Adelante, Siempre Adelante* (Onward, Ever Onward), and I've seen a copy in the educational museum in Montevideo—but I do not remember our efforts advancing me very far. Thus my joining the second grade must have been allowed more on hope than on achievement, for second-graders were competing in short-division races while I was still seeing how high I could count. Certainly I was befuddled, but not, that I can remember, frightened, and entirely to the credit of the Miss Paytons, by third grade I, too, was winning a share of races, now of long division. But my truly proud moment was being asked to stand up and read before the whole class a very long composition. Crandon was bilingual, half the day in English, the other in Spanish; I was the only English-speaking child in my class, and this composition came in the Spanish half of the day. I don't remember my story—the characters were dolls I think—but I still feel the astonishment of all that this reading meant. In my new language, new literacy, even a "new" life when I might well have been dead, I was being told that there was something I'd done, of my own invention, that others might enjoy and profit from. It was at the University of Washington that I encountered that attitude toward learning once more.

It is too bad that the entire venture of schooling for so many children chiefly lies in showing them they are wrong, marking the wrong answers, not the right ones, setting the whole process up as a sport of "answers." I expect I could become a worse crank on the subject than Grandmother was about animal rights. What sets me off is not chickens in bottles, but spelling. I am a terrible speller; my parents despaired of me. A reading expert in seventh grade tested me on the 100 most commonly misspelled words, and I got all of them right, which deepened their despair. Every teacher right through graduate school swore she or he would not pass me in the course if I couldn't spell better than "that." Always it is implied that the cause must range from willfulness ("She has a fey attitude toward spelling which is endearing but hardly effective," wrote a teacher at the boarding school on a report home), through stupidity, to near moral depravity.

A misspelled word is a warning sign of low socioeconomic level, low brain power, and probably dubious character. The English painter known as Carrington was an unconforming speller in the extreme. Michael Holroyd in his biography of Lytton Strachey quotes from her letters, for Carrington loved Strachey and lived with him and his lover, her husband, for many years. Holroyd reproduces Carrington's spellings, with the effect of making whatever she writes look eccentric if not nearly demented. There is also, however, an edition of her letters by David Garnett, who "regularizes" the spelling, and the effect is astonishing; Carrington in these pages turns into a sensible, thoughtful, wise, witty, and altogether "normal" woman. As for me, I am told that if I really wanted to, if I looked words up, if I did goodness-knows-what, I too could spell. It does no good to say either that I'd look a word up if I knew it was misspelled, or how can I look it up if I don't know how to spell it. What nobody believes is that, like anyone else, I'd spell well if I could. However, there is one advantage a bad speller can enjoy: reading medieval literature is less troubling than it is for "good" spellers. I have heard that spelling badly can come from growing up with more than one language, or that it can be a sign of brain damage. (I'll take brain damage.)

What settled the spelling matter for me in my own mind was learning that regularized spelling was an invention of the eighteenth century for the convenience of printers. A sensible economic move, as it is much speedier to set type and to proofread if you can depend on any given word being spelled always in the same manner rather than according to the ear or eye of each author. With this possibly arcane bit of information, I stopped worrying, and word-processor spell-checkers in the present day all but mask the social handicap. I wish I could spell, I rather admire people who say they can. I think it's nice to be good at it, but now I trouble myself very little that I do it badly. In teaching, I encourage students to spell as well as possible (although I probably don't often know it if they don't). I tell them it is convenient to spell well, but it is not an achievement of morality or intellect, it does not signal process of thought. It is also useful to know the multiplication tables, in spite of the prevalence of pocket calculators, but there is a difference, for knowing how to multiply gives one some entry into a general understanding

SCHOOL

of mathematics. The spelling of an English word, on the other hand, reveals little more than the spelling of that word. It does not flower into revealing many principles of the language. It is really too bad, as I say, that so much time and effort and shame still are devoted to making accurate spelling something worth achieving.

    I dwell on the question of spelling because it strikes me as an apt example of the unnecessary mystification and mortification of schooling, the persistent irrelevant punishment for not knowing. Yet how do we begin winding our way out of the physical confusions, the obliterations of personality that hardly stop with childhood? I stood one afternoon in my grandmother's bedroom, in front of a calendar on her dresser, staring at large numerals 1-9-3-9. I would have been seven years old, and it was occurring to me at that moment for the first time that that was the number of the year we were living in. Years had numbers, time was counted—something suddenly made sense. My son Stephen, when he was three years old, showed me another such illumination. He was playing with the Teddy bear that had been mine and was missing both its shoe-button eyes. "Teddy bear can't see," he said. Then he paused. "Because," he said, "Teddy bear has no eyes." Until that evening—we were finishing supper and he had got down from the table, replenished with vitality—Stephen would have set the two observations side by side: the bear can't see, the bear has no eyes. He had not yet said a word like "because." Listening to him, I grasped what I never really had from linguistics or psychology or even literature, how definitively thought travels through grammar (in contrast, obviously, to spelling). Stephen had subordinated one detail to another, he had realized a relationship and found the word to express it. For me, his "because" was a marker like the hint about date and time from my grandmother's calendar.

Lucky children are the ones who have been noted by someone. I was a lucky child—noted, paid attention to, not quizzed but conversed with by my grandfather Lockwood, my mother's father who lived in Tucson. He was the one member of the family with slight renown, however limited to Arizona and Tucson. When people referred to "Dr. Lockwood," I'd hear a slight bow in their voice. Fortunately, when I first knew him I was too young to be impressed, and later, if found to be "Dr. Lockwood's granddaughter," the connection appeared too distant to make much difference (although my mother and aunt complained of the burden of his notoriety). What was important and I expect crucial in my growing up was his letting me know—how that happens, like falling in love, one can really never tell—that he took me seriously and expected the same in return. Of course he was fond of me; he was charmed by children generally. As Mother shows, he doted on all his grandchildren, and on the visit to Tucson when I was seven, he'd watch me roller skate and skip rope by the hour. But for me there was more: he saw me into a future is the best I can explain it, in a way I had not detected from other adults I knew and had not so far had the imagination, or courage, to foresee for myself.

When the grandchildren were little, he was the grandfather anyone could idolize. He made stilts for us, and bows and arrows capped with empty shotgun shells so we wouldn't hurt anything we might hit. He'd throw a rubber ball over the roof from the front of the house to the back, even though my grandmother said not to because it was sure to go down the chimney, and when one day it did, there was the smell of burning rubber, though no wrath from my grandmother. He'd take us to the campus, and we'd roll down the small knoll in the lawn in front of the library building, and with a boost from him in his shirt sleeves, climb into olive trees (I see notices now that they are not to be climbed). On one of the Foreign Service leaves we were in Tucson at graduation, and our grandfather, in deanly garb, halted the entire academic procession to greet us.

Frank C. Lockwood taught American Literature at the Univer-

III

SCHOOL

sity of Arizona from the time of the First World War until the late 1930s. The walls of his study were full of books. He wanted me to have some of them he told me; he said they'd be useful when I went to college. I was living with the Lockwoods then and going to school in Tucson, and at that point in my life a promotion from ninth grade to the first year of high school was about the limit of my aspirations. College was another planet. Nevertheless, he had me pencil my initials on the flyleaves of anthologies and literary histories, and while none of these volumes actually came my way, I sensed something new in his offering them. It was not a present (the way he never failed to mark a grandchild's birthday with a book), but a gesture toward my responsibility for myself.

As long as I was with the Lockwoods, every afternoon when I came home from school my grandfather expected "scintillating conversation"—his words—and I had better scintillate. He would be propped up on blue pillows on a daybed in his study, a room just off the hallway. He faced the front door, so there was no hope of slipping into the house out of his gaze. He was always there, expecting me—white mustache, black eyebrows, and white hair rising in two arches away from the part down the middle of his skull. At over six feet, he was tall for his generation, he stood very straight, and he looked long on the couch, his feet to the edge even as he was half sitting, the soles of the leather slippers wiggling at me when I came into the room. Along the few blocks to my grandparents' house from Roskruge Junior High School, I rehearsed what might be salvaged from Spanish class with Miss Ott, who I thought was wonderful, or physical education with Miss McTavish, who graded me no better than C in volleyball, about which my father opined, "No McTavish / Was ever lavish." It was not easy to scintillate on such thin fare, but as my grandfather evidently thought my day worth hearing about and adding to his, I could not very well let him down.

Conversation, if not uniformly scintillating, was—or my grandparents' at least—usually interesting. Both had grown up among farming families in Kansas. My grandmother had been a student in a class he taught at the college in Beloit, Kansas, and they liked to tell of his turning over the buggy on a ride when they were courting. Grandfather's father was a Methodist circuit preacher—there were stories of prairie fires when, in horse and buggy on his circuit, he'd start a fire ahead of himself to stop the one coming from behind. When he was eighteen, my grandfather had a job as a newspaper reporter and was sent to interview Boston Corbett, the man who shot the man who shot Lincoln. He discovered him, when the elder Lockwood let him out on a country road, in a dugout. His report of that nervous call—a gun and a Bible ("trusty sword of the spirit" it was described) were the man's only visible possessions—is the piece of writing of his I am fondest of. He had stories of his days in the WCTU when in Carrie Adams fashion he preached in bars against demon rum. (On the other hand, he always asked, but never was told, what was the secret ingredient in the cake my grandmother made that he liked so well, which she could never present as her rum cake.) His manner of telling a story, of filling us in to times that now are a century away, comes back to me in one of his letters to Mother, when evidently she had asked for accounts of his youth:

> In 1876, in my 13th year, I broke down in school—a very serious nervous trouble, Chorea, or "St. Vitus Dance." It was thought that my undue application in school, helping to prepare a school exhibit for the Centennial in Phil, brought on this nervous breakdown. Dr. Enoch Moore, of Decatur, Ill, married one of Papa's sisters, which one I do not remember. It was thought that a change, and Uncle Doctor's skill would work my cure. So I went and lived with him for 3 months, and he gave me electric treatments. I was entirely cured. I had a very happy time there. Uncle Doctor was then a widower—the oldest, best-loved doctor in the city. He lived in a large two-story brick house, with a lovely lawn, where we practiced archery. He wore a plug hat, a chin beard, a double-breasted black coat, and was lame in one leg, limping along with a cane. His sister, Mrs. Gray, kept house for him;

and she and her daughter Emma and I had very pleasant evenings playing Authors, or reading.

Order and peace and quiet reigned in the Lockwood household when I lived there (sometimes to my stupefaction on interminable Sunday afternoons). People came to call, and listening to the conversations on the front porch was always interesting. Jeff Milton, who had been a Texas Ranger, was nearly blind by then, and would be led up the porch steps by Mrs. Milton. (When he became ill and was taken to the hospital shortly before he died, he insisted on carrying his shotgun with him, and as I heard the story, kept it under his pillow.) The men would make themselves comfortable in the wicker porch chairs, then Jeff Milton routinely offered my grandfather the silver whisky flask out of his pocket, which my grandfather would just as politely decline, and they'd get down to conversation.

I do not remember ever hearing my grandfather irritable or angry. The one time I saw his feelings roused was an evening when my grandmother had gone to friends to play cards, and my grandfather, on his couch, began a very long saga of the terrible campus warfare twenty years earlier, about cronies who met late at night on the front lawn, fighting for their academic principles against the university president, who had the backing of the state governor and all Arizona newspapers. The story went on and on, for after all those years, my grandfather was still enraged. Then he motioned me to bring him two pills from the top drawer of the desk, a glass of water, and said I should go down the street for the doctor, as he was having a heart attack. He was a passionate man in his convictions and affections, but temperamentally easy going and not self-absorbed.

He was good at finding pleasures. In travels by train around the state, he took with him a valise of horse-shoe pitching equipment and would set up stakes while he waited for trains, his object the company of local citizens and other travelers who a horse-shoe pitch was bound to attract. In a new city, he'd ride buses to the end of the line and back, and advised me to do the same, which I have, and he took me on bus rides in Tucson, pointing out where city walls had been. So used was I to thinking him the most contented of men that I have been surprised to find in passages in letters to Mother a more somber view of himself, of a man disappointed for having neglected to do what, as far as I can see, would have been much less worthwhile than what he did devote himself to.

He valued most the books he wrote, the best of them on Arizona history, on early settlers and the beginnings of Tucson, on Father Kino and the Spanish missions, yet to Mother he wrote he felt he had achieved little in them. He takes me aback with the vehemence with which he rebukes himself. At a time when he was urging Mother to begin writing (while we were in Washington, in the early 1940s), and to discipline herself to continue, he gave her advice on approaching publishers, processes that evidently reminded him of how difficult they had been for him. This train of thought led him to conclude that he had accomplished much less than he hoped. It is not only the strong tone of his disappointment that surprises me, but what I'd consider a misunderstanding of his own talents:

> I made two mistakes due to ignorance and lack of confidence in my own qualities. I should have gone in for a literary life—the career of a writer when I was 21; and at 40 when I wrote my first book; and still more at 64 when I began my series of Arizona biographical and historical books, I should have realized that I wrote well enough to do something really worth while. Thirty-five years ago—at least 15 years ago—I should have applied my talent, such as it is, to a biographical figure of world significance: Wordsworth, for example, or some really great American. I now know that both my scholarship and style would have been adequate to associate my name permanently with said world figure. I do not want you to make a similar mistake if you enjoy writing, and intend to do a good deal of it; for your gifts

are quite equal to mine; and your original, or creative powers greater, I think. So aim high; and do not allow yourself to think poorly of your possibilities of achievement.

Certainly Frank C. Lockwood's books on Arizona history have been followed by scholarly works that are more exactly detailed, more conforming to current historical scholarship. Yet his informal travels around the state, horse-shoe pitches at the ready, practiced the oral history that in our time has become as acceptable as manuscript research. He was one of the first to show that Arizona *had* a history, and the sense I gained from him was that although the state was young, it was no history its inhabitants should be ashamed of. Perhaps his judgment of himself is little more than the very ordinary feeling I easily share that whatever thing it is one is able to do, it cannot be very important precisely because one has managed to do it. Only things that are difficult and nearly unattainable, and probably not much fun, our Calvinist heritage tells us, are deserving. Worth is measured by difficulty and disappointment. Yet my grandfather was not dour or puritanical, and he gave no sign of rejecting a good time, which is why my analysis does not convince me, for he enjoyed too much a morning on the porch with Jeff Milton.

What if he had indeed applied his talent to a biographical figure of world significance? During the academic year 1909—1910, the Lockwood family, including my mother who was four and her sister two years younger, took the year away from Meadville and traveled to England. They followed the haunts of Wordsworth and the romantic poets in Grasmere and the Lake country, and then went to Oxford to attend lectures by George Saintsbury and other literary scholars. If ever Frank Lockwood were to have advanced a strictly academic scholarly career, I should have thought this would have been the time. He kept a journal day by day of his observations (I have it among some miscellaneous papers, although most of his manuscripts are at the University of Arizona Historical Society), and from these and an article or two based on the journal, it appears to me that his interests in Grasmere were very similar to those in Arizona. He responded to the land, the countryside, and most warmly of all to the people he met, but the poetry of William Wordsworth, as I read him discussing it, sounds to me as out of his reach as he decided it was from the shepherds and shopkeepers who told him they had not read it. After visiting Dove Cottage:

> I am a good deal of a hero-worshiper, and it is difficult to describe my feelings as I went in and out of these low, quaint little flag-floored rooms, and that of the great souls who lived their simple lives there, and thought their great thoughts there. Guests had been entertained in these crude little rooms whose names will be famous for centuries throughout the world. Here were letters in the handwriting of these far-away intimately known Wordsworths, and many pictures of W and Dorothy. The very bed in which W slept, the very chair in which they sat. It is impressive, too, to see of how little consequence they were in the sight of their neighbors; and are to this day to the dwellers here about.

My grandfather could not say enough to praise Grasmere: "We are pleased here with everything. Every expectation is satisfied and more than satisfied. The beauty, majesty and variety of scenery about here it seems to me cannot be surpassed; then there is the spirit of Wordsworth continually pervading everything." He walked up the steep Easedale road: "One does not know anything about the real fascination and wonder of this region until he looks down and around from one of these heights. It can only be felt and not described; and besides we have Wordsworth, so no details." Looking for the "spirit of Wordsworth" by way of peoples' actual connections to him, he sounded a little vexed: "In the morning I got a shave at Grasmere's only barber shop. It cost me 3d. It was done pretty crudely in a little bicycle repair shop, shaving being merely

SCHOOL

an accessory. I asked the barber whether there were any intelligent residents in Grasmere who were familiar with W's poetry, and who knew about him and were interested in telling some of the traditions of W in this region. He said he hardly knew. He said there were some people who knew about him, but that he did not know of anybody who read his poetry." At Hawkshead he "went into the room where W lodged as a boy; and talked a long time with the present proprietor. I am going to try to spend a night in the room Wordsworth occupied as a boy," having walked, he estimated that day, 18 or 20 miles.

Early one morning he went to a place called Easedale Tarn from which he could see crags reflected in the lake water, and there arrived a little closer to the Wordsworth he was looking for:

> The old shepherd had not yet come up, but I met him on the way as I went down, and chatted with him awhile. He said he had seen Wordsworth when he was a boy of 7 or 8. He said the children were afraid of him as he was a very solemn man. He said he wore the plainest and "rustiest" clothes. The shepherd Mr. Wilson was born in the Swan Inn. He said that Coleridge and W had luncheon there before they climbed Helvellyn, and that his mother served them. I asked him if he knew anyone in Grasmere who was fond of W's poetry and would be interested. He said "Really I do not know of anyone." People around here do not care about his poetry. It is very little read.

The journal continues:

> Wed. Sept. 29. This has been another memorable day. The sun rose bright and warm, and up to ten o'clock, the day was as beautiful as any we have had. At 9 o'clock we all started out to see Laucrigg, the beautiful place made memorable by W and Wm. and Fletcher. The estate is now owned by Mr. Roby, a retired Cambridge professor. He is absent, but at Miss Richardson's suggestion we made application to the gardener, and he allowed us the perfect liberty of the grounds, and we spent the whole morning there in a continual state of excite-

ment and delight . . . Helm Crag juts above; Seat Sandal, Stone Artin and Fay Free to the left, Silver Horn, and the other mountains to the right and in front, and Easedale back to the right. There are points higher up on the terrace where W used to walk and compose his poems where a still more extended and ? view is to be had, but from no place is the total effect more ravishing than from the walks and lawns directly in front of the house. Just above the house and a little way back toward Far Easedale is the terrace where W composed the Prelude and many other of his most perfect and memorable poems. The present owner has erected a tablet in honor of Dorothy W, at about the spot where she used to sit and transcribe his poetry. The gardener was very kind, and cut me a walking stick of holly from the prog of the very seed W planted with his own hand. It was one of the happiest moments of our lives.

The Lockwoods' departure from the environs of Grasmere was as romantic as any of their days before: "This afternoon at 1:30 we set out for Hawkshead, and by previous arrangement are spending the night in the house Wordsworth roomed in, when as a boy, he went to school here in Hawkshead. I am to sleep to-night, in the room Wordsworth occupied during his school days here." The Lockwood family left Hawkshead the next morning for Oxford.

Who am I to say that my grandfather was better off doing what he did than continuing to traipse the haunts of Wordsworth? His journals evoke for me the Methodist enthusiasm with which the Romantic poets evidently were still regarded a generation or two after their deaths. Nevertheless, the attention in the journals seems to me to be to the side of literature (even allowing that my grandfather's time and mine have rather differing interests in criticism). Wordsworth's spirit, let alone the poetry, sound more distant than are the barber, the shepherd, and other men and women my grandfather so engagingly talked with.

At the end of my stay in Tucson, school let out for the summer and I returned to the ranch. The day I left, my grandmother called

SCHOOL

a taxi to take me to the bus station. My bag was ready by the door, the taxi waiting, and I a little nervous about even such a simple journey by myself. The Lockwoods, like my own family, were not ones to exaggerate leave-takings. My grandmother had packed a lunch, and kissed me. I reached my arms around my grandfather, at about his lower rib cage, and then felt myself held with more force than I supposed he had, or I had felt from anyone before. The taxi honked, but he did not move for the longest time.

CHILDREN

AT THE BIRTH OF EACH CHILD, I entered a hospital prepared to die. That sounds ridiculously melodramatic—all the pregnancies were uncomplicated and the resulting children uniformly healthy. Nevertheless, the look in people's eyes when I was discoverably pregnant let me think they feared the possibility that I might die and wanted no part of it; they were writing me off. (Of course, birth puts both child and mother at risk, and over time there have been casualties enough, but I do not think my acquaintances had this history in mind.) The interest of doctors and nurses was the same as women have always complained of: counting pounds and centimeters, to the exclusion of the experience I felt I was going through. For me, each child became an ally in defying the odds of mortality and in surviving the oddities of hospitals.

The nurse who brought in Sarah once she was born said I might look, but would not trust me to hold her. Waiting for Sarah, I read Blake, my imagination gratefully lost in his visionary epics. Yet my own brush with religion held far less conviction. Richard had put me down on an admittance form as having a religious preference for the Episcopalian. This indiscretion resulted in a bedside call from a man of that cloth, who explained arrangements for the service in the Prayer Book called "Churching of Women." I've looked it up: "The Thanksgiving of Women after Child-birth, commonly called the Churching of Women" (*Book of Common Prayer*, 1928 edition, pp. 305–307). Opening rubrics read, "The Woman, at the usual time after her delivery, shall come into the Church decently appareled, and there shall kneel down in some convenient place, as hath been accustomed, or as the Ordinary shall direct," and "The Minister shall then say unto her, 'Forasmuch as it hath pleased Almighty God, of his goodness, to give you safe deliverance, and to preserve you in the great danger of Child-birth; you shall therefore give hearty thanks unto God, and say,' ". . . Psalm 65, in which the relevant verse must be, "I found trouble and heaviness; then called I upon the Name of the Lord; O Lord, I beseech thee, deliver my soul." Next the Minister recites the Lord's Prayer, the short version, through the words "deliver us from evil," followed by this exchange:

> Minister: O Lord, save this woman thy servant.
> Answer: Who putteth her trust in thee.
> Minister: Be thou to her a strong tower.
> Answer: From the face of her enemy.
> Minister: Lord hear our prayer.
> Answer: And let our cry come unto thee.

After that, the Minister thanks Almighty God for having been "graciously pleased to preserve, through the great pain and peril of child-birth, this woman, thy servant, who desireth now to offer her praises and thanksgivings unto thee." I suppose the minister is picking up on the suggestion of the psalmist: "What reward shall I give unto the Lord for all the benefits that he hath done unto me? . . . I will pay my vows now in the presence of all his people, in the courts of the Lord's house; even in the midst of thee, O Jerusalem." In any event, the last rubric states: "The Woman, that cometh to give her Thanks, must offer accustomed offerings, which shall be applied by the Minister and the Church-wardens to the relief of

CHILDREN

distressed women in child-bed." The bedside visit should have produced cash.

True, during junior high school, when I had been with my grandparents in Tucson, I attended Young People's Fellowship meetings at the nearby Episcopal Church. I liked being with the other kids, and I liked the music on Sundays, and laying embroidered cloths on the altar seemed useful and pleasant. But my episcopal enthusiasm was short-lived. I attended a church camp one summer, my grandfather generously having paid the fees, despite the dim view he himself took of Episcopalians, simply because, I feel sure, he could see I was eager to go. Sometime during the week I fell into conversation with Bishop Kinsolving, who told me, I remember well, that women were not allowed to be bishops. I lost interest—not that I really wanted to be a bishop, it was the idea of being told I could not. Now in the hospital, declining to be "churched," and asking Richard please to prefer no religions for me in the future, and probably not very decently appareled, I wondered who was this "enemy" fomenting pain and peril? Death, of course, as I'd always suspected; and the reward expected from that "strong tower" of an Almighty God was no surprise either: money, albeit for the "relief of distressed women in child-bed."

It may not be fair to criticize the rather stiff language that makes the ceremony sound like an embarrassment all around. In almost every other respect, I think the Book of Common Prayer, along with the King James Bible, is a literary work crucial to the ear of anyone wishing to know our literature. But this service strengthened my hunch that pregnancy was thought a harbinger of death. Goodness knows one feels grateful when the child is safely born, but the obligation to be readmitted into a community that I had not thought I'd left, strikes me as strange. "The Woman" evidently is alone; the service mentions no family, friends, or even a husband (and only at the end includes an optional prayer on behalf of "the child of this thy servant"). The woman and the minister both read the psalm, but only he recites the Lord's Prayer, surely the central text for Christians. Most dispiriting to me is an absence of joy in this service. It hardly evokes the very real elation one cannot help feeling when a child is born, a profound euphoria of gratitude that I think indeed does have claims to religious experience. It goes without saying that pregnancy can be uncomfortable, one can at times feel miserable, many women suffer acutely, and some die. The moment of birth is painful. But surely all is not "trouble and heaviness," nor the outcome entirely a route of enemy dangers and distresses. Birthing women are made to sound guilty of something, or at war.

Stephen was born in a vast university teaching hospital in Columbus, Ohio, so brutally efficient that he was ejected by a doctor's plunging his fists above my belly until I felt him hit the spine. Stephen was brought to me in blue tissue paper, confirming the enormous incongruity at each birth between tawdry, slick surroundings and a happiness that fairly took my breath away. The incongruities were not mine alone. The woman in the next bed, when she was gathering up her belongings to go home, had to insist that the child brought to her in tissue paper was not hers, and that it be exchanged for the one who was. Her bed was taken by a woman who described working as a beautician, which she liked, and her husband, who she said she did not. She could not wait, she said, to have her tubes tied. At night I listened to women crying for having had another child. For myself, I was pretty sure if the baby and I could exit with our wits about us, we'd easily stick together for life.

Over the tub in the bathroom in our house in Columbus, Richard constructed a plywood shelf for changing diapers; it was on ropes and could be fastened against the wall when the tub was in use. One morning, Stephen, seventeen months old, had been put into fresh diapers and clean clothes, and set down from the shelf. He ran the length of the hall, but neglecting to stop at the top of the stairs, fell to the iron furnace grill at the bottom. He was unhurt, yet the shock to my system evidently was enough to make that night the one for Andrew to be born. Richard had gone to a party, and I was sorry to have to telephone and interrupt, as well as extricate another couple who came to stay with Sarah and Stephen. There was a nice moment, though, while I sat in the kitchen waiting for the others, and told Sarah (age four), who had not yet gone to bed, that I was going to the hospital to have a baby. She said, "And Daddy will say what a beautiful baby"—which he did, and he was.

There is an expression I like in the French translation of *Anna Karenina* describing the conditions of the Oblonski household when the father has been discovered to be having an affair with the children's nursemaid: "La maison Oblonski était bouleversée" (the Oblonski household was in confusion). "Bouleversée" was the condition of the Methodist hospital we went to with Andrew. It had recently opened and was reputed to be less frenetic about childbirth than most hospitals, in days before relatively natural childbirth was widely practiced. At least fathers were allowed to hang about this one. The labor room was equipped with an intercom, the speaker on the wall. When it appeared to me that someone had better start paying attention, I pushed the button, and a donald-duck voice said: "What do you want?" Richard asked me, "Well, what do you want?"

In the delivery room when I got there, rather ill-tempered people were standing at wall sinks washing their hands. I was lying on what felt like a narrow metal rack with an open space just beyond the hips, and listening to the people at the sinks saying what an inconvenient moment this was, between shifts. I could observe in a mirror above me that a head with a great deal of dark hair was hanging over that break in the rack. It was Andrew's, and I suppose someone rescued the rest of him. He was being wiped up at one of the sinks when the doctor came into the room, breathless and sounding cross, with Richard behind him. I heard the doctor ask about anesthetic. "I put a little here, and a little there," a young man said, pointing rather vaguely, although I am pretty sure no one had come near me before Andrew was preparing himself for a dive to the floor.

I thought I had better not laugh, but I wanted to: at the ridiculous scene, and because of the joy that, again, overcame me, the elation at birth matched by nothing else I can think of. Only this time there was more to make me laugh. At the actual instant that Andrew was slipping out, my wince from the usual pain was confounded by the quite contradictory sensation of orgasm. I could not have been more astonished, though I supposed, thank goodness, none of the men fussing about could have noticed. Later, after Richard and I had laughed in happiness together in the ward, trying not to waken other sleepers, and he had gone, I realized there were acute pains in my abdomen, but not from childbirth. I was hungry. "Labor" is not called that inaccurately. I meandered down the hall until I found someone to ask whether I might have something to eat, and was brought a piece of dry toast and small bowl of gelatin.

David was born our second winter in Grand Forks. Andrew had started kindergarten, and there were three months of mornings with no child in the house. I was teaching, and although this was the late sixties, the University of North Dakota still had few women on the faculty, and only one, by repute, who ever had appeared in the classroom pregnant.

We went to England by ship that summer (renting a house in Cambridge where my sister Felicia and her husband and children were living and teaching at the technical institute), and I managed to be seasick even when the ship was at anchor. Only between midnight and 1:00 A.M. did I come alive. Then Richard and I would walk around and around the decks, the barriers separating second- from first-class sections being down at that hour. The ship dining room served what they called Irish tea, which I think meant it had been boiled. It was thick and black and truly vile, but was what mainly sustained me. The rest of the summer went well, all of us bicycled the environs of Cambridgeshire, and when I returned in the fall to teaching, I planned better than usual the due dates for student papers—I would read them in the hospital over Thanksgiving vacation, I hoped. But David demurred until long after students were returned their papers.

At the end of the last week of fall semester classes, there came a critical college faculty meeting, critical to the dean at least, who had been lining his ducks up for a vote. His and our families had been friends since the days in Columbus, it was they who had stood vigil when Andrew was born, and they had persuaded Richard and me to come to Grand Forks. Certainly I was prepared to vote for the cause (removing a language requirement I think it was). So there I was, in the chemistry lecture hall with others who were teaching the arts and the sciences, and myself feeling ominous disturbances. Then home to fix supper and watch the others eat, and while it was being discussed which child's turn it was to wash dishes, allowed as to how we might go to the hospital. This one was merely across the street. I could see the children's bedroom windows from my own room and know when their lights were out and they had been put to bed.

All went well. It was a Catholic hospital with frocked nuns on the late-night shift who did not mind a chat if one weren't sleeping. I was home in a couple of days, but on David's third day, there began fierce pains in the abdomen. Take two aspirins and go to bed, they said when I called the number I'd been given "if you have any problems." The problem was, I tried to explain, that swallowing anything made the pain worse. No female complaint, this, although I did not have energy to argue long. A doctor came eventually. I could see the idea growing on him as to what the outcome eventually would be if I neither ate nor drank again, and I was sent back across the street. Children were parceled out, and a surgeon corrected for a second time the intestines folding in on themselves that had occurred in Montevideo when I was a child.

Where this episode affected David's birth, or his early days at least, was with regard to the milk supply. Modern hospitals are too specialized to pay attention to more than one body part at a time. Someone had bound cloths tightly around my chest, and staff was pleased that no milk was leaking by the time I left. But the thought of bottle-washing depressed me. The wife of a friend of Richard's was a devotee of the then-popular nutritionist Adele Davis, and when Sarah was born had urged on me "tiger's milk" (brewer's yeast in tomato juice), which then I did not need. Once back at home and the children collected, Richard went off for brewer's yeast and a can of tomato juice, and I started downing the awful stuff. But it worked, and before a week was out, David was off bottles and back to mother's milk, and I, I confess, rather pleased with myself. (The pediatrician at the one-month checkup visit looked appalled.) None of the children, as a matter of fact, ever learned to suck from a bottle, so that my leaving a clean one with a can of powdered milk to ease the minds of baby-sitters was uniformly fraudulent. David had a friend his age who would come to the house, bottle in hand. David liked to take the bottle away from him, put the nipple between his teeth, and wander around with the bottle hanging below his jaw, and no idea what else to do with it. I thought it time to stop nursing when he remarked one day, "Um, good."

Our fifth child and fourth in birth order is Mary Ann, adopted when David was four years old and she seven. She was born in Bumble Bee, Texas, and was living with a foster family in Victoria, Texas. Her parents had come to Texas from Mexico. In the 1970s, Texas still forbade "mixed" adoptions; children of Mexican heritage could not be adopted by non-Mexicans. Nevertheless, adoptions were being sought for such children and they were being sent out of the state. (Native Americans and other non-Anglo-Saxon ethnic groups had not yet become politically active in favor of keeping children within their group, as began to be the case a few years later.) Negotiations for the adoption of Mary Ann made me glad Richard was spending the summer at a pottery workshop in Northern California, because only the conviction that adopting a child was a good thing to do and that we were likely to be an adequate family kept me at it. Our social worker had received from the Texas state welfare offices a printed catalogue containing pictures and descriptions of various children. I paged through and picked Mary Ann. She arrived in the care of a social worker, and was carrying a doll that was bigger than she was. The doll had been given to her by a public health nurse, a Miss Scott, all of which I took as a good sign. The catalogue had described Mary Ann's hair as blonde, a somewhat special attribute among brown- or black-haired Mexicans; it was in a rather lanky ponytail. But once I cut and washed it, her hair turned wavy and dark as her eyes.

The day the family, all seven of us by now, gathered around a long table in a judge's chambers to formalize Mary Ann's adoption, the judge asked me in what year each of the children was born. I had to say I did not know, he should ask them, which he did, and they told him. Of course I remember when they were born, I insist to the children, I just don't know what year it was, or even, sometimes, how old they are. And they know I am apt to call any one child by the name of one of the others, as I remember Mother used to rush through all four of ours whenever she wanted any one of us. We knew who we were, she'd say, and now I see her point. Mary Ann herself did rather better. Her school went to the university campus art gallery one morning, where the children took it as a major event to sign the guest book. It happened to be the day when the governor of North Dakota was on campus to confer ROTC commissions. Moving up in line toward the guest book, Mary Ann asked the man behind her how to spell Hampsten. It was the governor, William Guy, she was speaking to, and puzzled as he may have been, I am impressed that after only a month with us, she knew her new last name.

Who are these people who filled thirty years of my life, yet whose birth years don't stick in my mind? Day by day what does stick is the blur of unclothed, diapered bodies moiling about on hot Ohio afternoons; mounds of stews and spaghetti sauce and beans and chili dished up supper after supper; clothing gathered up, whirled through a machine, and put away, the cycle seemingly never stopped. There is little to mystify in the day-by-day materialities of food and clothes, voices in and out of the house, the precarious fending off of absolute disorder, the charm of it all and the exhaustion. It is as though, over years with one's children, there is nothing we can escape knowing about them, at the same time as they, and the connections between us, grow more mysterious.

When parents speak of their children, at least the parents and children I know, they seem to feel it more permissible to complain than to brag about the brats, as though visibly to rejoice, or show simple wonderment, might appear sentimental and embarrassing (or maybe bad luck). I can only suppose that we are inhibiting each other from pronouncing a source of almost universal joy: I'll qualify it that much in deference to the hospital cries I have heard in the night. Or, an unkind sign of the times, that to show enthusiasm for children may place us with those who use the word "family" to signify a back-to-the-apron-strings doom for women. For all sorts of reasons, children, the beings we must know best, are difficult to speak about.

If we do dwell on childhood, it is more likely to be our own. We make guesses about our mothers' and fathers' lives together, although actually our understanding is more likely to center on what our parents "did" to us. I have less sense of how people I know think about their own children. Most obviously, they concern themselves with problems: birth defects, allergies, sequences of colds and diseases, high or low school grades, good or bad tempers. The conversations of parents run to children's sleeping through the night, toilet training, learning to ride a bicycle or drive a car, the colleges that have accepted them, the jobs and professions they dedicate themselves toward. But once each crisis is over, I wonder how far conversations lead past those single accomplishments or shortcomings. The mysteries within our children, the elation they bring as well as anxiety and paying of bills, these seem to me we should also, and more often, be willing to speak of. The experience of my children in time is both different from, and a variation of, my own; they are bound to know years beyond what I will, yet elements of their lifetimes, with luck, also will be continuous with mine.

The first house Sarah lived in, and the first for Richard and me together, was a farm house overlooking Green Lake in Seattle, where through a slit between the two houses beside us we could glimpse Mount Tom in the Cascades. By spring Sarah lay under the rowan tree outside the door, amusing herself with the red baubles dangling above her, and before long learning to roll over and slither among a patch of marigolds. She refused to walk alone until one evening the fit hit her, and at a run she circled dervish-like between a bookcase and three walls, round and round unable to stop, Richard and I laughing, thrilled and appalled.

Columbus was where we had three infants in an adequate but not especially attractive house—a "half double" on the shotgun plan (front and back door three rooms apart but in line with each other, so presumably one could shoot from the one door through to the other). Richard taught in the Ohio State English department, I taught part time, and both of us worked at completing our dissertations at the University of Washington. When I achieved more chapters than children, I thought I might make it. Columbus holds for me strangely disorienting images. Even as we drove into the town—after the journey from Seattle, drawing a trailer with our goods, camping, Sarah in her buggy top—I knew right away, block after block down High Street, that I was only waiting to leave. It had not occurred to me how truly one could detest a place, but from the first I loathed everything about Columbus. It looked to me an ugly and angry town. Two rivers join there, but instead of being given to parks and lanes, their banks turned into rutted motorcycle runs, and one was warned not to walk there—although I did; we were near the river and there was nowhere else to take the children. A child in the next house (the street was lined with doubles) often came at noon to the door for money for hamburger for lunch, she'd say. No social services appeared to be attending to the family, which I realized had moved one night, carting their goods in a child's red wagon, and taking our borrowed flashlight. These were years of civil rights marches, to which the main newspaper, the *Columbus Dispatch*, responded by publishing names and addresses of persons joining those marches, a convenience not lost on anyone who wanted to throw trash on their lawns. A woman was murdered two blocks from us. There was a funeral establishment at the end of the block. One evening, on the way to the grocery store across High Street, as I walked across the parking lot, a light in a window on the third floor drew my glance. Exactly framed in the light was a raised arm holding an ax.

Columbus was where James Thurber had grown up, vigorously hating the town. I read all I could find of him over again. It comforted me that he noticed the women on busses with pursed, thin lips. His essay "University Days," about Ohio State, is so widely anthologized in composition texts I had it almost memorized, but even so I was not prepared for how accurate was Thurber's eye and ear. The botany professor, the one who insists the then half-blind Thurber "will too" see something besides milk through a microscope, was a man Thurber tells us who "liked flars." The day we began moving in to our half-double the landlady came by to chat.

CHILDREN

Richard asked her whether she'd mind if we planted a few things in the back yard. O, she said, she "just loved flars." I had to leave her to Richard for fear I'd laugh out loud at a Thurber character appeared in the flesh. Thurber had died a short time before, and to honor his memory the city of Columbus was naming its first shopping mall Thurber Village. Mrs. Thurber came for the occasion, and the *Dispatch* reported, with no irony in the writing, that she said she thought James Thurber would have appreciated that.

My "look-out" in Columbus was to try not to turn into a Thurber character myself. What with a new place, new jobs, new acquaintances, and two new babies, much of my ingenuity went to warding off small disasters. I invariably smelled of cheese. Even my lying in bed on bath towels did not keep milk from seeping through and rotting the mattress. The wife of the chairman of the English department once a year invited wives of department faculty to her house for luncheon. I had come with the wife of Richard's office mate to one of these to do my bit as faculty wife, fortified with extra padding and a jacket in a heavy weave. If I did not let myself think about Andrew, I hoped the milk would stay put. All went well until we were at the door to leave, when our hostess asked me, "How's the baby?" and then stared as the front of my suit darkened before her eyes. My friend yanked me and we fled.

For the first couple of years in Columbus, I did not teach. Richard and I had agreed there were three things we each wanted to do: finish dissertations, teach, and care for the children; but either of us could do only two of them at a time. So until dissertations were finished, he would teach and I would mainly look after the children. When Sarah was three, I started what I called a nursery school of half a dozen three-year-olds who came to the house a couple of mornings a week. They provided a little sociability for Sarah and Stephen, and enough income for me to buy a set of blocks and a wooden train. With Andrew and Stephen and a graham-cracker supply in the baby buggy, and the three-year-olds holding on to the buggy sides, we'd make our way to some of the less motorcycle-infested grassy parts of the river bank. The nursery school also gave me anecdotes for academic cocktail parties, but nearly cost me a start on the freshman composition career ladder. The dissertation finished, I applied for part-time teaching and made an appointment with the chairman. It was an oddly strained interview, until I realized that he was trying to tell me with painful courtesy that a nursery school for three-year-olds did not in itself qualify me for teaching freshman composition.

Small children prove how precarious is the status of adult, how tenuous a hold the mind has over matter. Matter, in these years, was everywhere: pots and pans on the kitchen floor and children inside the cupboards, my lap never empty when I sat down nor my hip free of a child when I stood up. It could be an existence of exhaustion and despair. It is hard, still, not to think I betray the children I so want to do well by. I know nevertheless I felt them an enormous pleasure even in that almost undifferentiated state of diapers and spilled cups, of the terrible crying, merciful silences, and, amazingly, the soft sounds of their preoccupied small noises. Few parents probably can keep up to the wit of their children, and I expect we had no better than average luck at being taken in by their mischief. One evening in Grand Forks, all of them had been put to bed in the care of kindly Mrs. Froehlich, and Richard and I set out for a party. We had hardly driven to the end of the block when one of us remembered the loaf of bread I had baked that we intended to take along. I went back into the house, to find Sarah, Stephen and Andrew (ages ten to five) lined up at the kitchen counter beside Mrs. Froehlich, who was slicing bread still warm from the oven. The children had explained to her, she said, that they always had a slice of bread after they went to bed.

The part I valued most of my own growing up, the "best years" you might say, were of course the eleven when we were on the Double A. I consider the ranch my parents' inspired gift to me (we

CHILDREN

were all most of the time enthusiastic, but I know less in particular about how those years affected my sister and brothers). Parents must hope for that, that each child will have been especially touched by an experience of the parents' devising, although I do not suppose these can be plotted with much accuracy. Mother and Shiras had the general idea that country living would be good for their tribe, but the specifics of how a ranch would affect each of us they could have had no way of judging exactly: any one of us might have hated it.

Conversely, sometimes things we look on rather casually may turn out to have special importance to one child or another. Richard and I enjoy camping. I never had camped—ranching was close enough to it for my parents—but by the mid-fifties camping was becoming an increasingly popular, low-cost form of travel and recreation. National parks were expanding and improving their facilities, tents still were made of canvas but equipment was getting lighter and more efficient, and gasoline was cheap. Richard and I would go camping and hiking in the mountains around Seattle, taking turns tying Sarah to our back with a flannel blanket (baby-carriers were still a few years away). By the time we reached Grand Forks we were a fairly adept camping family. The best camping in North Dakota is at the Theodore Roosevelt National Memorial Park, North Unit (try saying all of that in one breath as the children did), and we set up the tent there fairly often, under cottonwood trees at a bend of the Missouri River, and hiked the Park Service trails. Then a few years ago, Stephen and I, just the two of us, found ourselves setting up a tent, his this time, under the same trees. Stephen had completed a course for chefs at a technical institute as well as several years of restaurant cooking in Madison, Wisconsin, and was on his way, by car, to find work in Seattle. I made part of the trip with him, and we stopped for a couple of nights at Theodore Roosevelt National Monument, North Unit. We did the nature walk, and one or two longer ones, and Stephen cooked and I mostly sat around using the water he'd boiled up in cups of tea, and realizing that it was possible to camp without a diaper pail. It dawned on me as well that Stephen was experiencing something of a return to important parts of his childhood, that our sometimes rather frenetic excursions had settled themselves well in his memory. He loved the park, he said, and often thought about what it was like to be there.

At the time, I do not think I considered Richard's and my launching into the venture of a school as anything comparable to the Morris family on the Double A, but now that I do think of it, there may be some parallels. For the seven years the Open Community School lasted, it was certainly all-consuming for our family, and I expect it formed our children to degrees beyond what I'd be able to appreciate. These were the days of experiments in "open" education, and also a time when the university had received a federal grant that brought about an added New School of Behavioral Studies to improve public education in North Dakota. Several New School staff and students as well as others were enough interested in putting into practice their academic experience to launch the difficult venture of a parent-run and -financed school approved to grade eight.

For my part, I was feeling considerable desperation that our children were set to repeat the same fear, the boredom, the constant escapes from shame that I endured through so many years of schooling. To be sure I had also experienced satisfactions, but they came later, I thought, than they need have, and I dreaded the process all over again for our children. For a number of years we rather drifted along on hope—that a school would turn out to be not too bad, that a good teacher would show up. And indeed, now and then, so it happened. Jiminy Crickets, a primary school in Victoria, British Columbia, did not do too badly by Sarah and Stephen for the two years we were in Victoria. In Grand Forks, Stephen's first-grade teacher was the gifted, intellectually alive teacher every child (and parent) dreams of. Sarah's sixth grade was put through the paces of a court trial, for which Sarah was the defense lawyer, and while she lost her case, the whole classroom was clearly animated by the exercise.

But for the most part, while the public schools in Grand Forks were hardly abusive, I realized they were giving our children little to remember. Truly, "nothing" happened, and it was the thought of the years of vacant memories they'd be left with that made me nearly frantic. Sarah was sent to the principal's office as a troublemaker for pointing out an error in a history text. Calls were coming from Andrew's kindergarten teacher that he was standing up and walking around when he was supposed to sit. Parent-teacher conferences were a torture: Stephen's second-grade teacher had written a list of things he did wrong: he stared out the window, he didn't color inside the lines, he read the wrong books. Then she said, "And besides, he's so small." Starting the Open Community School (OCS)—the year Sarah was in seventh grade and David approaching kindergarten—appeared an imperative against all of that.

OCS lasted seven years. A history of the school would narrate a complicated mix of idealism of the late sixties with hard common sense and practicality: the principal also was head janitor. The fiercest arguments during all-school meetings were not about ideology or curriculum but about cleanup—whose turn it was, and why was it not done better. The school hired one teacher, and parents taught as much as they could. Richard was treasurer most of those years, the person best suited in the group to keep a measure of order to what we were about. My contribution was The Peanut Game, which started the youngest children reading, urged on with peanuts that left a mess but concentrated their minds wonderfully.

OCS children, nearly everyone agreed, learned how to learn. They learned how to talk with each other and with adults. They developed a grace and ease about themselves that many of us as parents could be in awe of. They also seemed to have picked up a lot of information, even though appearances, to an outsider, might seem otherwise. Even after the school closed, when the beginning group of children outgrew the school at the same time as interest in alternative education had waned too much to attract new families, it seemed to most of us that our children were too well equipped, too surely on their way to their own education, to be seriously hampered by other schools, as I think indeed has proved the case. The academic effect on our particular children may have been more radical than on most others: of the five, David is the only one so far to have attempted a college degree (with something of the pioneering attitude of first-generation sons of immigrants), and he and Mary Ann after their first seven years at OCS were the only ones of the five to experience a conventional high school. The State of North Dakota requires school attendance until age sixteen, and completion of the eighth grade, but nothing is said about having to move on through higher grades. Sarah, Stephen, and Andrew remained for several years in OCS eighth grade and enrolled in some university courses at the same time, then went on to other things: Sarah to farm and family in Wisconsin, Andrew to the Olympic Cycling Camp in Colorado Springs, and Stephen to restaurant work in Madison. The house was full of books, the university campus their backyard, and it was as though, or so it has seemed to me, these particular children neither needed nor wanted any more of classrooms.

How Richard's and my children did settle on what they did mystifies me. If their choices have had an element of doing anything else except what might be related to their parents' occupations, obviously they have succeeded. On the other hand, when I see what they do, and watch them at it, it makes me ache, because their man-

CHILDREN

ners of working and living repeat so much my own manner, and I expect Richard's as well. In some respects they continue obvious family habits. With my memories of falling out of four-poster beds at Dingleton, I persuaded Richard that no one would suffer that trauma if all of us slept on mattresses on the floor, which, until the house got so crowded we had to put up bunk beds, everybody did. Now in Sarah's house there also are mattresses on the floor, and when I visit Andrew, he arranges a futon for me on the rug. But it is not only specific habits a scattered family keeps in common. Annoying mannerisms, flashes of temper, prejudices and paranoias, it is easy to trace an inheritance of faults and vices. (Andrew could blame his bad spelling on me, and I on my father, who was not quite as bad but not a whole lot better).

Yet it must be the same for some more attractive characteristics: as I watch the carefulness with which they work, and the care they give to their relationships with friends, lovers, their own children, I know these children of Richard's and mine are behaving in manners I have most admired in Richard, and in better moments, can think I strive for myself. Mary Ann's being moved from one family to another cannot have been easy for her; as a terrible teenager she did not resist saying now and then that if she were living with her real mother, she would be much happier. After high school, she completed a secretarial course and has been working in an office full time. She is married, with two young daughters. She also has made connections with her mother, who sews in a garment factory, as well as with several sisters who also grew up in adoption or foster care, and she visits them in Texas. Mary Ann seems to be the one who mainly is re-tying that family to one another.

There is an indefinable sense of family among our children, made visible when one might least expect it. A poet visiting the campus in Grand Forks came to dinner at our house; Richard and I had known him as a fellow student in graduate school. The five children were at the table, listening politely to his telling of books he'd published, readings he'd been invited to, the prestigious job his wife held, the music and dance and language lessons of his children, a trip to Europe the family had taken. Stephen, then eleven, asked how many children did he have? Three. "Only three," Stephen murmured sadly.

Bicycles qualify in our family taxonomy—there were eleven in the garage one year. At the turn of the twentieth century, and before the full day of the automobile, the bicycle, I think it has been said, began the social revolution in transportation, and it was the bicycle that established rules of the road, such as driving on the right hand side in two-way traffic. Bicycles certainly must be the vehicles of maximum independence, as long as one has the strength and skill to ride and does not contemplate very long distances. If it is true that the bicycle is the machine best proportioned to the human body, as I have also heard, then it is not surprising that on a bicycle one can feel so well complemented, so close to complete, you might say. Carlos Liscano is a Uruguayan poet, now living in Stockholm, who spent thirteen years of the Uruguayan dictatorship in the prison Libertad. One of the poems he wrote in prison commemorates his experience through an appreciation of the bicycle.

> *La libertad es una bicicleta.*
> *La libertad es una tortuga.*
> *La noche es la libertad*
>   *donde todo es posible.*
> *La libertad es una tortuga*
>   *en bicicleta*
> *atravesando la noche.*
> Liberty is a bicycle.
> Liberty is a turtle.

CHILDREN

> The night is liberty
>   when anything is possible.
> Liberty is a turtle
>   on a bicycle
> going through the night.*

    Bicycles have been the vehicles with which our children learned to move themselves. There was a summer the family spent in Cambridge, England, when Stephen and Andrew came into their own as both cyclists and travelers. Richard took the boys to Italy while the younger children and I stayed in Cambridge, and in addition to churches and monuments, they visited Italian factories and bicycle shops. Richard negotiated the language for them, but returned impressed, he told me, by the questions the boys had him put to proprietors. In addition, it was not long before Stephen and Andrew were the ones figuring out train connections and taking charge of luggage. When I saw them again in Cambridge, they had a traveled air about them.

    Soon after, Andrew wanted to see a bicycle fair in Manchester, which the rest of us were not keen about. He persuaded us to let him go alone on the train (he was fourteen), spend the day at the fair, and return the same night, which, though exhausted, he accomplished. At such fairs, various manufacturers display bicycles they claim have been ridden by noted cyclists. At one stand Andrew realized that the bicycle on display was actually made up of parts from several companies, but when he unfortunately pointed out the fact to the proprietor, he was thrown out of the fair. In Cambridge, Andrew and Stephen made themselves acquainted with the local cycle shop, where the proprietor organized races for the neighborhood boys, and even made up teams he transported to races in

---

*Carlos Liscano. *Estará no más cargada de futuro?*, p. 11. Montevideo: Vintén Editor. May 1989, #12.)

London. These cycling friends would come to our house speaking the Cambridgeshire dialect I could barely follow but the children delighted to imitate.

Grand Forks is a town obsessed with ice hockey and the university's notorious hockey team. Toddlers skate almost before they walk. Richard and the children enjoyed cross-country skiing in the parks, but I do not think the children often skated. When we first moved to Grand Forks, apart from children, I hardly saw anyone on a bicycle. Thus Stephen and Andrew's interest in serious cycling took solitary devotion—training rides with a few older boys and help from a father of friends who coached and organized training rides. But the more serious they became, Andrew especially, the more long rides they made alone. In the mid-seventies when the rest of the country was rediscovering bicycles and bicycle racing, races had a brief vogue in Grand Forks, and once some riders came from Winnipeg for a race around the campus drive. Stephen and Andrew, along with Peter, in the family of friends from Columbus days, entered the junior division (the three made up the entire junior division). Stephen came in first, Peter second, and Andrew, then thirteen, third—in birth order. Peter and Stephen have not let Andrew, since then a contender in international races, forget that once they beat him.

Mobility is commonly associated with freedom and independence, but it has taken my watching our children to appreciate how that should be so. I began to see that while they were getting themselves from one place to another on a bicycle, they also were learning the subtle courtesies that can smooth along movement and mobility. On a bicycle you know how much space you take up, you locate yourself in relation to other fixed and moving objects. A similar spatial sense must be at work as one travels among various and differing environments, geographical, physical, and cultural. It looks to me as if our children have that sense, whatever it is, that is certainly crucial to independence, or to Liscano's liberty. (In an interview, Carlos Liscano described the trauma of leaving prison that others have reported as well; he had forgotten how to open doors, he said, or buy bus tickets or go shopping, and for a while his sister had to guide him about.) When Mother found me contented in Flagstaff, I expect she felt I was experiencing something of that liberty, or I hope she did.

It is a liberty hardly come by easily, but I may have found a way to help our children gain a little of it on the domestic front. When David was four and going to OCS with the others, and also tall enough to see above the kitchen counters, I stopped serving breakfast to the five of them. That put a stop to whining for eggs the mornings I cooked cereal, or the other way around. Breakfast materials were available in the cupboards and refrigerator, and everyone could have whatever she or he wanted, but they were to fix it themselves and get to school on time. Inaugurating this self-service regime may have been my single most sensible child-rearing tactic, for it launched each of the children on what I'd call their material independence. They were already fairly handy in the kitchen, helping to fix meals and often coming up with a cake or other treat themselves. They enjoy good food and are particular about what they eat (a racing official looked at me a little testily when she told me once how fussy Andrew was about what went into his food bag). Being on their own for breakfast gave the children practice in household management; when the last egg or cereal box or cup of pancake mix was gone, they knew they had better write the item on the marketing list or suffer reprisals from the next cook. Our kitchen is small and usually a mess, but on the whole domestic chores bumped along not too badly. I cooked dinner, and the children took turns washing dinner dishes. I washed up the day's accumulation of dishes before dinner, on the principle that neither chore is so bad if you don't have to do both for the same meal. The tyranny of housework that men impose on women has its origins, I'm convinced, in the fear anyone would feel at not knowing how to keep themselves alive day by day. It reassures me that the children in our household have an eye for grocery ads. As a matter of course, they put away dishes or sweep the kitchen floor or take out the garbage, doing what has to be done before they start the next meal because they are not baffled or fearful of the necessary rhythms of a household.

One thinks back through one's relations, rummaging as it were for the salvageable while trying to discard refuse. I can tie string around a paper parcel almost as well as Grandmother Morris, and while I lack her head for finances, I think I sometimes emulate her organizing abilities. Her fierceness lurks within me too, I suspect. I try harder to cultivate the Lockwood grandparents' genial goodness, their hospitality, their seriousness about books, inheritances I prize while falling short. My own parents I still view almost as cautionary figures. Their charm, their wit and intelligence, their kindness to friends and generosity and good intentions toward their children are qualities easy to admire, and yet as long as they were alive I do not think I ever felt unburdened by the worry of them, nor did I ever really achieve a simple, adult friendship with either. I rather think Charly, Fifi, and Pancho did (or I hope so) in travels with them to Europe, trips together to Mexico, and visits to Tucson.

Which leads me, naturally enough, to wonder what rummage collection I am relegating to my children. Seeing to it they did not fall out of bed I thought an obvious and simple improvement over my own upbringing, but after that, intentions become more complicated. It gratifies me that they seem to continue being good friends with each other and visit one another often. I also think I enjoy with each of them a much easier friendship than I did with my own parents. What I certainly have tried to avoid is having them feel oppressed by me. I promised myself long ago that if ever I had children, I would do almost anything not to have them anxious about me as I had been in the habit of being with Mother and Shiras. If somewhat ruefully, one episode encourages me to claim success. All the children were home during a summer when Richard had gone by himself to Europe for a month. The telephone rang one afternoon, and a child answered. (The story comes to me from a friend who had it from the caller, but will not tell me who that was nor which child she spoke with.)

"Is your father home?"
"No, he went to Europe."
"Is your mother home?"
"No."
"Did she go to Europe?"
"I don't know."

Common sense tells me that I am not altogether absent in my children's imaginations, but it remains a cautionary incident just the same. More often, the children surprise me in the ways they think of me. Andrew, for instance, told me once about an interview he had had for a cycling magazine. He'd been on a holiday in Utah, leisurely riding back roads with a miscellaneous group of cycling enthusiasts, including a woman who wanted to write an article, she told him, capturing the "real" Andrew. At breakfast, the journalist began by explaining how professional and strongly feminist she was, and that while she did not usually begin this way, she wanted to ask a few background questions. What did his father do? He taught English at the University of North Dakota, Andrew said. Did he have any brothers and sisters, and what did they do? "Wait a minute," Andrew said, and began a grin as he repeated the conversation to me, "Aren't you going to ask me what my mother does?" "All right, what does your mother do?" In the same, level tone: "She teaches English at the University of North Dakota." The journalist writes that she gave up the idea of pursuit, and produced a thoughtful article just following Andrew around for a few days.

The holiday group consisted of out-of-practice sporting goods executives, former racers, hangers-on, and a few current cyclists.

Stopped at the top of a long steep climb, they realized that one of the party had lagged so far behind he was nowhere to be seen. Andrew turned his bicycle around and went back down the road to find him. The rest were astonished, the article reports, that he should take such trouble. We talked a while about talent, how hard one works for whatever ability is at hand, yet how difficult apparently for others to know that that draws on the very ordinary as well as extraordinary. The quandary faces all the children. Being able to do something well should not deprive them of what Shiras liked to call the simple pleasures, nor simple decencies. With Andrew I certainly worry about his getting hurt. I make no effort to go to races, although Richard one year followed some of the Tour de France. I can barely endure watching television clips. How Andrew maneuvers the pressures of publicity, the constant travel between races, to say nothing of the social relationships among teammates, managers, coaches, and the rest, astonishes me even more. And I admire most of all his grace and good humor, how he quotes back to me Mother's line about having a lot to be modest about.

Or I think of a remark of Stephen's, another boy with a lot to be modest about. In Seattle he is chef in an Italian restaurant. On visits home, he is a wonder to have in the kitchen. He and I have concocted together some fairly impressive Christmas dinners. He can arrange tomato and cucumber slices on a plate that make you wish the plate were finer. Still, he surprises me. I often had made a lettuce, grapefruit, and avocado salad with little idea whether anyone liked it, only that it got eaten. In his technical institute cooking course, Stephen was to prepare an "American" meal as his final examination. He told me he served what his classmates thought was exotic: a salad of lettuce, grapefruit, and avocado.

While Stephen and Andrew were home one Christmas, we met with friends for lunch. The boys' enthusiasms for cooking and cycling provided adequate conversation for the sandwiches we were eating, and the meal and talk were winding down when someone asked Stephen what kind of cooking did he like best. He vaguely said he favored variety; like Andrew, Stephen stays away from personal questions. But friends persisted. Did he want to work in large restaurants or small? Was he partial to French, Italian, Czech, or some other national food? We were getting out of our chairs, gathering up coats and meal checks, and the quizzing might have dragged on a little tense. I wondered whether these friends were not really wanting to know why anyone would make his profession in kitchens. Then Stephen said, "I just want to cook like Mom."

As I write, all five children are in or past their twenties. Their friendships, with me and Richard and among each other, I'd try, but could never quite envision in the days of diapers and mashed bananas. Those experiences are over, but they form all of us, and we're bound to think of their passing with both fondness and relief. There will not be a return to the time, for instance, when I gazed absently at the lovely silhouettes of birds in a mobile the children had constructed. We are a frugal family, and they obediently confined their drawing and cutting-out to the back sides of used paper. The mobile was on a string, tacked to the ceiling above the table where I typed, a gesture that charmed me, until my eye focused on print I recognized. The birds were cut from sheets I had only recently been typing.

China

IN CHINESE CITIES, travel is by bus or bicycle, and buses are unbelievably crowded. When a bus stops at intervals of about a mile, one crowd presses to get in as another knot gropes its way from the inside out, neither budging for the other. If you get on, you stand pressed against everyone else, trying to protect children from the crush. "Erotic without being sexual" is Richard's expression for this intimate press of flesh. Bus No. 107 in Beijing serves the Friendship Hotel where Richard was living, and is distinguished in the *Guinness Book of Records* as the bus line, worldwide, that carries the most passengers. We stood on a curb late one evening to ride No. 107 home. It would be the last bus for the night, and it arrived at the stop empty: this was its starting point. The throng rushed in, and by the time I got my bearings, I saw no possibility of adding myself to the bodies already pressing out of the entry from inside. There I would remain, alone, somewhere in the middle of Beijing, never to be seen or heard from again. Then a hand, Richard's, emerged in the dark from between bodies, and I grabbed it, and felt the pneumatic doors fold me in.

But in our month in China together, Richard otherwise did not draw me toward himself. He was teaching English at one of the teachers' colleges, on leave from the University of North Dakota. I had stayed in Grand Forks. Our youngest child, David, at seventeen, was in high school, and the two of us kept an agreeable bachelor establishment. I had urged Richard to try teaching in China for a year. It always has gladdened me that we have done unusual things together or apart, but I missed him. Richard had said he wanted a visit from us in August, the month allotted to him for travel. David and I both were a little dubious about going to China. What we were reading about daily conditions, even in 1985 when it was still government policy to welcome foreigners, did not make the country sound that inviting, and we knew nothing of the language. But Richard was insistent that we come, and so we went. Yet once arrived, it turned out we were an intrusion. No matter how small a pile I made of my belongings behind a door, Richard could not stop complaining about the "mess."

It was easy to see why. His accommodations in Building H of the Friendship Hotel were comfortable, and by Chinese standards luxurious. He had more space to himself than any family apartment he took me to visit. There was a sitting room with two chairs, a desk, bookcase, and chest of drawers; a bedroom with two single beds, cupboard, and coat stand; a bathroom with tub, sink, and profusely leaking flush toilet; and kitchen with a sink, cabinet, and clothesline, where he did no cooking, although some people arranged charcoal burning stoves in theirs. Hot drinking water was brought by custodians in two thermos bottles. Richard would take the cork out of one thermos to cool the water enough for brushing teeth, and keep it in the other to make tea (leaves in the cup, warm water added throughout the day). Someone came to sweep and dust, and once a week laundry was picked up and delivered. In these rooms Richard had been living in as perfect comfort as he may ever yet have found. There was a glassed-in shelf for the knickknacks people gave him, and playing cards of actors' masks were lined up under glass on the desktop. The ugly wallpaper was almost masked by scroll paintings also given to him. Small drawers with individualized compartments kept his socks and handkerchiefs. Here

CHINA

I could see the harbor he'd constructed from the domestic disruptions of nearly thirty years.

Even so, these weeks in China could not help but be fascinating to me. For someone as enamored of bicycles as I am, this was bicycle heaven; the country is run by bicycle. One very hot day a fan went past me, upright and whirring, somehow attached to a rear carrier. The basic model in manufacture is the heavy, black bicycle popular in England about the time of the First World War, and its advent in China must have been an event of incalculable significance. Farmers bring produce to the city on bicycles from as far away as fifty or sixty miles. Workers commute twenty miles or more within the city, and people use their bicycles for every kind of errand. Several hundred bicycles may be packed into a parking lot, all looking to me exactly alike, yet each distinguished to its owner by a lock, a basket, a rag behind the seat, or some other small individuality. An industrial model, built a little longer than standard, is fitted with enormous panniers astride front and rear wheel, and may pull a platform trailer. These, or tricycles with a platform over the rear wheels, loaded with lumber, a sofa, a refrigerator, or bales of waste paper four or five feet high, become as good as trucks. I saw children stretched out on mats on these platforms, asleep in the midst of traffic. In the western city of Kunming a young girl every morning passed along the street where we were staying, riding a tricycle loaded with charcoal briquettes, while her younger brother riding his bicycle alongside helped push hers up the hill. Bicycles are attached to wheelchairs; someone sits pedaling on a seat either before or behind the person in the chair, or the rider may propel his own three-wheeler by means of a hand crank attached to handle bars.

Richard acquired bicycles for both David and me, and we joined the throngs, I gripping handlebars with white knuckles. We cycled, it seemed enormous distances, through the sprawling city in a pack of cyclists that was constant and unremitting. The pack moves slowly and steadily. Almost no one races through the press, but neither does anyone give way. I learned, as in a school of fish, to focus on no single object, yet not loose the feel of the flow. Once, I made the mistake of slowing down, intending to stop because an elderly woman was trying to cross this river of wheels with an enormously loaded cart. As more and more machines eddied about me, I realized my intentions were threatening mayhem, and gave up. I had no better luck on another point of etiquette: it is considered polite to ride side by side, the better to carry on conversations, which move along, like the press of wheels, quietly and constantly. I never managed that. I thought myself lucky just to keep up, or if I truly got behind, spot David's light-brown, curly head above the throng and weave toward it. Negotiating a second lateral dimension was beyond my powers.

Beijing is laid out in wide straight avenues and three ring roads, presumably for military advantages. Cars, buses, trucks, and taxis use the center lanes, as well as new Japanese or German automobiles, going at a good clip and often curtained in the back, where one assumes are sitting the party powerful. Everything else—pedestrians, pushcarts, horse and donkey carts, and the bicycles—moves on wide lanes to the side. Motorized traffic, though light, travels quickly, and sometimes recklessly. Right-of-way apparently is determined by size and speed of vehicle. One night, crossing on my bicycle on a green light, I very nearly did not reach the other side for an army truck coming toward me on a quick left turn.

Since the government returned to killing and imprisoning in June of 1989, much of what I had experienced four years earlier may well be gone. Then the talk had been of the depredations of the first Cultural Revolution—flower plots dug up for vegetable gardens, but few, in the evidently brief respite, restored to flowers. Yet even in those halcyon days, the country made me feel sad: the monochromatic colorlessness of concrete high rises, the endless walls hiding whatever might be interesting behind them, the dark blue or gray pants and skirts so many wore, with white shirts hanging loose and hiding any body shape. Houses were dark at night, and undecorated. Except for the traditional costumes of native people, or the institutional renovations of parks, temples and other monuments, I could see little evidence of what I would call efforts to make daily surroundings more beautiful or comfortable. Public parks and Buddhist temples were always crowded with Chinese on their days off, but these places felt to me disassociated from the life outside their gates. They are referred to as "scenic spots," as though imagined separate from the rest of the landscape, confirming its sad drabness. People smiled in a polite way, but I did not see many laugh.

The Beijing art museum, where I went several times while Richard was doing other errands, gave me a little idea of how the country might have become more hospitable to itself. The building, except for some tropical plantings at the entrance, was not inviting. The ubiquitous cement walls and three floors of unbroken open spaces where paintings hung one after another evoked more the appearance of a warehouse than a gallery. But there were refreshing surprises. The first floor was given to traditional scroll paintings. On the second were oil canvases in the style of socialist realism and U.S. magazine covers. One charmed me: five or six women at a health clinic, sitting in a row on a bench waiting their turn, each with an infant, dandling, nursing, wiping a bottom. The third floor exhibited art touched by Western European and American painting (bookstores carried reproductions of famous European art works). A canvas I admired, perhaps two feet square, showed a white sky, the scalloped edge of a tile roof, and several small birds on the tiles, the whole exactly blending Chinese and Western styles.

The paintings in this museum, to the extent that each was the work of an individual artist, were different from scroll paintings seen in shops. Student friends of Richard's took us to a painting factory that produced commercial scroll paintings. Here artisans made the paintings, mounted them with silk onto scrolls, and manufactured the shipping boxes. We were introduced to the master painter, the one person who did individualized work. While we watched, he painted a sheaf of peonies in the traditional style, wide brush strokes of red and black, and presented it to me, because peonies are considered female images. In the same workroom sat a dozen or so others producing what the factory mostly turned out, copies of older paintings. These men and women were copying by hand, sometimes from torn ancient papers or silks, each design, every wash, every line and detail achingly exact, with cotton-tipped swabs and the smallest brushes, mathematically replicating the original. I asked one young woman working flower petals on silk how long it had taken her to learn to do that. Ten years, she said. A silk factory we visited probably typified industrial labor, employing the system invented in Britain in the eighteenth century, a precursor to computer punch cards. Workers sat on stools at keyboards punching holes into cards that represented every thread of a pattern. Each card gave notations for a single row of weaving, and the cards joined on a belt to direct the thus partly automated looms. The light was dim, the noise very loud.

    People worked all the time at tasks that looked physically exhausting and highly particularized, everyone doing a small action over and over. There was construction everywhere, although badly planned, an architecture student told me, for highways were being designed in the paths of new high rises. Few machines were in use. Women as well as men carried bricks and cement in baskets on sticks across their shoulders, and lifted bundles of bricks on pulleys to the tops of buildings. They wore woven reed helmets. Amazing to me was bamboo scaffolding rising five or six stories, the joints tied together with reeds. The work in offices, what few I sat in to wait, appeared slow. Telephones worked sporadically, mails were slow, few typewriters were in evidence. People seemed to be trying to be helpful, but complications were nearly endless. Buying a railway ticket could take an entire day, and an airline ticket several days, and sometimes would not be available at all. There was no assurance that requests to officials for what might seem routine services would materialize.

Much labor was given to sanitation. In the streets someone always was sweeping with broom branches, gathering watermelon rinds, cigarette ends, paper and other refuse into large piles. Except in parks, I saw almost no public trash cans that might have saved the trouble of some of that sweeping. Public toilets contained a long trench, sometimes tile, that someone must have had to scrape out (there was no running water). Stores carried stacks of fairly heavy paper as toilet paper or folded into sanitary napkins. The anti-spitting campaigns must have been enforced only sporadically, for spitting appeared socially acceptable. People spat at the dinner table, say, either onto the floor or on the table beside the plate. On our later train trip west, a woman came several times into our compartment to chat. She taught English at a university and was on her way across China to Beijing for a passport to visit in the United States. As she talked about her teaching and an American friend she was to visit, she spat from time to time on the carpeted compartment floor.

It was hot in Beijing while David and I were there, and the life of the city was in the streets. Outside the relatively parklike quiet of the walled compound of the Friendship Hotel, a different rhythm asserted itself on the boulevard divided by trees and plantings in the middle of a constant flow of buses and bicycles. On the other side—after a perilous cross—was a small market, post office, and general store. That summer individual sellers were doing so much business that the state stores, especially food stores, had few customers. There were rows of men's trousers spread on the ground, baskets of vegetables, the sweetest peaches I ever ate. On the fringe were tobacco sellers, shoe repairmen, and a bicycle repair station. At night, people sat on the city sidewalks, even on boulevards, reading by street light, playing cards and board games; they set beds under the trees for a cooler sleep than indoors.

Numbers are astonishing, and so is the youth of the population. Many who now would be in late middle age died in the war, and birth policies have made young children a rarity. And yet, although nearly everyone seemed to be in their twenties or early thirties, males and females behaved distantly toward one another. A girl riding on the back of a boy's bicycle, I was told, was considered to be engaged. I saw little of the casual intimacy one is used to in the West, no holding hands. But among same-sex couples, the situation was different. Women held hands or took each other's arms, as a woman who worked with Richard did with me one evening, walking us to a bus stop, rather as I used to walk with "best" girlfriends in the sixth grade. Men's public intimacy appeared to me more intense. Men, too, held hands, or went about with arms around each other. Men sat or stood close to one another, hands on arms or shoulders. It was not unusual, for instance, to see two rather tough-looking teen-age boys on a bus stroking each other's backs and necks. Homosexuality, however, was forbidden, and homosexuals reportedly were shot along with criminals.

The old and the young were said to be the best cared for. An old man told me happily, in English, of his quiet days, retired from teaching English. I was by myself in Sujo on our trip there, waiting while Richard and his student friends found a hotel room. I was standing with the luggage on a grassy strip in the middle of a full street, the only spot I could find not in the way of traffic. The man came over to me and talked for some time about what a good country China was for old people. One sees them attended to: a young girl of about twelve walking with a very old woman to a public toilet; children sitting with elderly people in parks or on front steps, it not being too clear who is minding whom. Babies, it was said, were spoiled, and indeed they looked always dressed very well, lines of little ones tied together by string being taken for walks—just as one views in tourist ads.

I asked a few people how they had learned English. One young man, who spoke well enough to be a guide for an American tourist company, said that when he worked on a collective farm during the Cultural Revolution, the one intellectual pleasure allowed was listening to English language lessons on the radio, which he had done avidly. Older people said they learned from missionaries, and in turn became the teachers of English in the schools. (Their English retained enough of what must be Chinese linguistic habits that I heard many say they found native speakers of English hard to understand. I learned to speak very slowly and distinctly, and was told, possibly out of politeness, that I was easier to understand than most Americans.) One young woman said a teacher in her village school had strongly urged her to learn English, and kept after her when she was considering dropping out of school. In Beijing there were "language corners" on the street, where on Sunday morning people gathered to practice speaking with foreigners in whatever language they were studying. On the street one might be stopped in the hope of a little practice. "Hello" was a word everyone knew and called out in friendly greeting, meaning one had been recognized as a foreigner.

Graduating university students were receiving their job assignments the week David and I arrived in Beijing, the universities having just closed for the summer. These jobs usually were teaching positions in secondary schools, most often in provincial towns far from Beijing. Almost all the students I met or heard of were unhappy. They wanted to remain in Beijing and to do almost anything else but teach. "Foreign trade" was their aspiration, although what that meant was never clear to me. A few used family political influence to achieve desirable work and locations, a strategy called "the back door" that appeared to be used frequently. On our return to the United States we used the back door ourselves through airport customs, with the assistance of a friend of a student of Richard's, and were saved from unwrapping every painted scroll Richard had been given. The back door appeared to be how things got done if they ever got done, regardless of anyone's offended egalitarian principles.

In China, it appeared to me, no one was ever alone if anyone could help it, a gregariousness due partly, I suppose, to the dense population, and also partly because everyone was watched. At the doorway to Richard's apartment building there always was someone sitting on a stool, to whom one said *ne-ha* while going through the hanging strings of beads that were supposed to keep out flies; and one said "ne-ha" also to the two young women standing at the door leading to the dining room. There were "watchers" in white tunics and red arm bands who sat on stools at the curb, outside shops, in parks, generally keeping an eye on things. Police wore green uniforms and red chevrons, and there were army personnel. I don't suppose anyone moved without someone's knowing it. On the grounds of a temple swarming with sightseers, I saw a young woman arrested for spitting, Beijing having inaugurated an anti-spitting ordinance. She was crying. Her husband stood behind her, his mouth stretched into a painful grin, smiling being a sign of embarrassment, while the white-smocked watcher scolded her long and loud. The young woman was fined the equivalent of a day's wages.

Richard thrived on the open affection students showed him. They crowded around him, even in his rooms as often as they could win passes through the hotel gates, and he returned this warmth (partly by arranging attendance at U.S. universities for several of them). He accepted gracefully their and their families' hospitality. His response to all the public regimentation was, sensibly enough, to try not to make a false step. But I was not prepared for how much attention he was paying to what people thought of him, and hence of David and me. At the end of a day he would tell us how we had done. I was finding his friends amiable enough, but the question of what people thought had not, to my knowledge, been something either Richard or I paid a lot of attention to. Now it was, and not helpful that I did not care.

I was awed from the start by the devotion he shows to that country. I could see that Chinese and foreigners alike marveled at his near fluency in one of the world's most difficult languages, and all warmed to the interest and respect he shows for China's history and culture. For Richard in 1985, China was exactly the right place to be at the right time in his life. It was as though he had found himself anew at home and in the midst of family, a spiritual and intellectual discovery of his that paralleled an emergence of Western sympathy for China. The Chinese may be inscrutable in our popular mythology, but at least in the mid-eighties, they appeared less malevolent than the Russians. While nasty reports persisted about criminals, homosexuals, and other "social undesirables" being summarily shot, and about female infants systematically murdered, these unpleasantnesses, in the minds of Chinese enthusiasts, did not match the gulags in the then–U.S.S.R. Ping-pong diplomacy had near magical effects in making China the new frontier not only for political and economic ventures, but for personal spiritual quests as well. China, undergoing brave new experiments in political and cultural re-education, in population control and economic development, in this new regard could hardly do wrong. In addition, China in 1985 was still one of the countries where English speech and an American passport held some of the aura that Americans used to take for granted but have seen erode in Latin America, the Middle East, and the African continent. Officially, the United States needs to be loved by China, and even after the disgraces of Tianamen Square, appears to be trying to restore mutual admiration.

CHINA

The excessive generosity of our Chinese hosts, to which Richard visibly responded with grace and appreciation, left me oppressed and bored. Two families, one with a son and the other a daughter at the University of North Dakota, invited us to dinner, a thirteen-course affair. The host couple were both engineers. Richard and I were each sat in rattan armchairs in the main room, next to a double bed and facing a television set that was showing what appeared to be a historical soap opera. There also were in the room a refrigerator, an electric fan, and a stereo. Walls were unpainted or stained green, and there was a calendar on one wall. Richard and I were brought refrigerated wet towels to wipe our faces, deliciously refreshing after the long cycle ride to get there. We were served lobster, a dozen other dishes, bowls of rice, watermelon, wines, and were constantly urged to eat more. Then came picture-taking. We lined up in various combinations, and after that watched television. At some point there was an exchange of gifts.

Richard had asked me to bring things from home, and I did, a suitcase full of sew-on patches, dinky toy cars, and comic books for children. There were boxes of gelatin and dry soup mix. From a thrift shop I scavenged T-shirts with the logos of the neighborhood elementary school, the university band, and a Lutheran Bible camp, in hopes they would be found amusing and not incur a sense of obligation. But I had judged wrong. Other people invariably gave us presents of considerable value: a pen and pencil set for David, a silk blouse and bottles of perfume for me, statuary and silk doilies with designs of the Great Wall for Richard. West School Viking T-shirts and gelatin boxes in this context turned out to be merely shabby.

Inept as I must have appeared to anyone attuned to Chinese culture, I was not so baffled as to miss the renaissance (or transformation) China was enacting upon Richard. To myself, I confessed to hubris: in all these years, the element in life's complications I had least worried over was our marriage. Richard and I were so used to one another I could not imagine either of our lives otherwise, or had not bothered to. No one appreciated each other's jokes as much as we did. China changed all that, but even so does not persuade me we had been mistaken in one another thirty years before, nor that the intervening years, for me at least, have not held riches.

Richard and I had had some classes together my first year in Seattle, but not a lot of sociability. Early the next fall, here he came through a doorway with books piled to his eyebrows on the way to return them to the library, and I thought, given the chance, this was someone I could happily spend the rest of my days with. When we arrived to be married at my parents' house in Tucson, I heard in the next room Mother exclaim to someone, "But he's nice!" I cannot think what she feared I would turn up with. The academic scene was less prepared for change. On our return from Tucson, the instructor in one seminar would not recognize me in class, and in another the man persisted in calling me "Miss Morris," until titters in the classroom motivated me to tell him that I'd been married since the last term and now my name was Hampsten. His answer was polite but the tone doleful: "Yes, I know," he said. Evidently I was a loss to serious scholarship, although Richard was receiving congratulations from the same professors. Richard learned to knit, and we'd each lay a board across an arm chair, prop up a book, and knit our way through volumes of *Shakespeare Quarterlies*. Sarah was born with a goodly supply of blankets and buntings. Our basement apartment in a farmhouse overlooking Seattle's Green Lake, with cherry trees in the back yard, first housed the rolltop oak desk we had found and bought at the vast St. Vincent de Paul outlet on the wharf. It would not fit either into Richard's room or my garage, which made us realize we'd have to rent a place, and so had better be married—there may be other unions begun as round-aboutly.

Richard introduced me to the Midwest. He accepted the offer of a job in Columbus, Ohio, he said, because the Midwest was "real," at least more so than the lotus land we'd given in to in the Northwest. (As Columbus got grimmer and grimmer, I had to stop reminding him how "real" the place was supposed to be.) During our four years at Ohio State, we often made the trip to his relations in Southern Illinois. Yale, the village where Richard was born, has probably changed little. He pointed out to me the upstairs window in the frame house where his birth had taken place, and I thought no wonder he can feel the Midwest as nearly a state of being. His mother had grown up in Fayetteville, Arkansas, and we could see why she spoke so nostalgically about the shady hilly town when we drove through it once. Richard's father was a butcher, and kept bees. The family (there are two sisters) had moved from Yale to Charleston, Illinois, when Richard was fifteen, but they still spoke about the move as though it had recently occurred, and the house in Charleston had a look of not being quite settled into. It was a family with many elderly relations: an aunt who had taught school, an uncle who farmed, and Richard's grandmother, who lived with his parents. She was thought of as somewhat ahead of her time. Divorced, she had supported the family during the Depression with an appointment in the Yale post office. Along with a Pepsi Cola scholarship, this grandmother had been Richard's main encouragement for going to college.

    This is the region that the novelist Hamline Garland calls the "Middle Border," not far south enough to be southern, but to an outsider's ear, the speech drawls. Some abandoned farmland has returned to woods or wetlands, and there is hunting again. It is the archetypal place of farms, small towns, screened front porches, and fundamentalist religion. Here is where you "prepare to meet your God." A cousin of Richard's mother came often for Sunday dinner with his wife and eight children. He was a minister in the Church of Christ, and he also sold a detergent he mixed himself. I'd listen to him on "Christ the Great Salesman," and wonder whether there was some blurring in his mind as to who was Christ and who the salesman.

I think now about these Illinois people. Richard removed himself away from them and into academic life as quickly as he could, yet like Garland, I do not expect he has really been that long away, even though the elderly all have died, and telephone calls and a few visits years apart have been the extent of his connections to his sisters. While we were in Columbus, Richard had gone to see his grandmother not long before she died. She had been the center of this family, something of a tyrant, I would have said, who Richard like the rest regarded with awe and fear. He had wanted me to admire the powers of her mind. But when he returned from the visit, he told me she insisted the Bible had been written in English, and nothing he said would convince her otherwise. Having held her as a model for his own intellectuality, her failing him at the last was a blow to him, I think.

Richard's absorption has been intellectual: in literature, philosophy, philology, linguistics, and all the languages he's learned—French, German, Latin, Ancient and Modern Greek, Italian, Spanish, Dutch, Welsh, Japanese, (I may have forgotten some) and now Chinese. It is his present preoccupation with the language and culture of China, and his friendships with Chinese university students, that I wonder are not bringing him back to the Edenic communities like Yale, where he gathered May apples along roadways and cooked dandelion and polk "greens," where his father brought home fried rinds called "chitlins" from the butcher shop, and where hours of conversation with his sisters, his parents, his aunts, and his uncles were exhibitions of total recall about who was related to whom and what they had done with themselves.

These are the communions he belongs to, I think, whether in Illinois or China, but ones I have little room in. Whatever may be that affinity to place and people that so mystifies me, Richard appears to possess it. Southern Illinois he was bound to leave (for all the reasons Garland did), but I doubt he ever stopped feeling the loss. Now, wedded to China, the void is filling up, and it is my tough luck, I tell myself sardonically, to be left aside.

After David and I had been a week in Beijing, there began the trip to the west Richard had planned. A student from Mongolia traveled with us and others joined later—it was a way for them to see their own country, and they helped with translation. We flew first to Shanghai, then went by train to Suzhou (Sujo), by canal boat to Hangzhou (Hanjo), then by train for three days to the western mountain city of Kunming, and back by train to Beijing for another week before David and I flew home, Richard returning some weeks later. The trip showed us scenes so pervasive in Chinese painting: the misty mountains, young children tending water buffalo, women and men under conical bamboo hats planting and transplanting rice sprouts from one geometric plot to another, the terraced mountain sides of rice, then corn, then squash in the least hospitable terrain, every foot in use. Junks on the rivers and canals had yellow ducks aboard exactly like the illustrations in the children's book *Ping*, but boats made of cement I had not seen before, families living as well as traveling on them. From a distance, villages looked painterly, all the buildings in a given locale made of the same material, the roofs identical.

The journey demonstrated as well China's careful class distinctions, through which Richard maneuvered delicately. Hotels are segregated by race: hotels for foreigners, hotels for "overseas" Chinese (people from Hong Kong, Taiwan, and those who had lived a while abroad), and hotels for mainland Chinese, the cheapest and least comfortable. Because we were traveling with students, it sometimes took the better part of a day to find places we could all stay together, the likeliest being hotels for the overseas Chinese, amenable to bending the rules. (Other public accommodations also acknowledged class divisions; in large restaurants service gets better, food more varied, and prices higher as one goes up the floors.)

On the train itself, you might say that all of China was present, massively in miniature. Again the socioeconomic divisions: "hard seats" meant two wooden benches facing a table between, for six; "soft seats" added a pad on the seat and white cloth on the table; "hard sleepers" were compartments with four bunks and a rattan mat; and "soft sleepers," where rode foreigners and the wealthier Chinese, provided a thin mattress, sheet, and blanket, as well as a small table with white cloth and cups and hot-water service. There was music blaring periodically through a speaker that in our compartment David muffled with blankets. The squat toilet, as the train lurched along, was a challenge. The train stopped every eight or ten hours, and crowds rushed out of the coach cars, where evidently there were not washing facilities, to a bank of sinks. There with their white towels people washed themselves, always on the run to get a spot at a spigot and back to the train on time. At one stop a dozen children tumbled down an embankment with watermelons to sell. After several minutes of brisk trade, a woman who had bought a melon had it snatched away from her by the white-coated guard of our car, and then a uniformed policeman took it away from the guard, shouting at the children, who by then had disappeared over the embankment.

Student friends of Richard's who met us at various cities along the way never ceased their attentions in their desire to express gratitude to him. We were taken to one scenic spot after another: to temples, tombs, and parks; to the painting factory; to elaborate and lengthy meals; we walked and cycled great distances. It is not polite in China to leave guests alone, ever, and we never were. My few attempts at escape from constant attention were considered aberrant, if I sat by myself under a fig tree in some temple grounds, or alone on a bench along a path. One afternoon David and I were wearied nearly to tears, so Richard suggested we rest in the hotel instead of visiting another scenic spot. The students were disappointed but cheerful about it. Three or four young men came with us to the room Richard, David, and I shared; they washed up, one or two took a shower, and then they stretched out where they found room on the beds or on the floor. We might rest, but not be separated from them.

Another morning, David announced that he was not going on that day's excursion to the Buddhist site. He wanted to walk around the large lake that bordered the city, by himself. The Chinese students begged me not to let him. He would get lost, they said, and he couldn't speak Chinese. I pointed out that there was no need for him to speak to anyone if he was going to walk, and he could hardly get lost going fifteen miles around a lake. Our hosts did not recover from their alarm until they saw David, solitary and considerably refreshed, on the hotel steps when we returned.

Much of the pleasure Chinese people evidently were deriving in excursions to scenic spots came from taking pictures of each other. The subjects posed carefully. I watched a young woman adjust some willow branches just above her. Richard took a picture of one of the students who wanted to stand in profile at an arched window. David took a picture of a whole line of people aiming cameras at their companions in front of a temple bell. We went to a temple in Kunming. On the grounds were tea houses and ponds and exotic plantings among the walks. I was tired. While the group of men took tea in the tea house, I sat on a rock by the pond to stare into the middle distance. A young couple came toward me. He was carrying a camera, and she said "Hello." I said hello, and the young woman sat beside me on the rock. She put an arm around my waist, the young man took a picture. Then, laughing, they left. I was their scenic spot.

Kunming is in the mountains, in southwestern China, near enough to the Vietnamese border to have considerable military traf-

CHINA

fic. But it is cooler there, a little misty. Richard thought it might remind me of Flagstaff, which it did. It even seemed to me a little more festive than Beijing; some houses had small murals painted on an outside wall. One afternoon Richard agreed that he and I would do some errands, our first moment on this trip unescorted by a crowd. We walked to the center of the city and bought a bag of dried mushrooms Richard wanted to take back to Grand Forks. We had tea in a cafe. We had been apart a year, and, while as I've said I urged him on his ventures, I missed his company a great deal when he was away. I could tell, though, that whatever he was finding in China by now meant more to him than Grand Forks (where he complains about the weather, the dull landscape, and dull people). In China he looked happy and serene, as though his surroundings exactly suited him. Across from me at the tea table, Richard asked me what I thought of China. I said I thought it was a sad country, I felt sad being there. He said I was mistaken. I could not think where a conversation could go from there, my sorrow greater for his China being so far from mine.

Sarah

T HE BENCH SARAH SAT ON was two rows in front of mine, in the presence of a district court of Madison, Wisconsin, where judge and jury were to decide whether or not she should be entrusted with the upbringing of her younger son, Ariel, age seven. The children's father did not want to be involved in the fracas; no one was even sure where he was. An aunt, the father's sister, had taken Ariel in from time to time and now was claiming him for good, saying Sarah was unfit. The aunt felt she had even stronger claims on his older brother, Ole, whom she had cared for almost continually from birth. Both little boys were more truly parents to each other and desperate not to be separated. Sarah was married now and wanting a fresh start, but, I wondered—feeling humiliated and pained and awed at how she was conducting herself, all at the same time—how had such a state of affairs come to pass?

It could partly be explained as an ordinary 1970s disgrace: a teenage runaway, two infants, no money. Sarah had been sixteen, in college in Montana, when she telephoned one Sunday in March to say that she and her friend Bob were going "on the road." She would not say where. Except for a card from California about herding goats, no word came until July, from Madison, when Ole was born. The man she was with had grown up on a farm near Grand Forks and had been a student at the university (a rather listless one, even, in a class I taught). They could be seen about the campus, arms around each other's waists, Sarah sweeping him along. She had fallen in love with Bob, with hitchhiking on the open road, with primitive living and very hard work. The two truck-gardened and sold produce in the Madison Saturday markets, and they lived in what had been an abandoned farmhouse, where both children were born.

For me those months had been an interval of such pain that I did not know if I'd recover, even should she reappear. I was sure nothing worse could happen, surely nothing could happen to me that was as bad as harm to one of the children—and I am still convinced of that, including the loss of marriage. I hardly think I drove her to it, nor could see how I might have prevented her. Little enthusiasm as I could feel for her choice, I was pretty sure that trying to forbid her seeing Bob would lead to something like what, of course, happened anyway. If anything, I empathized; (except for the goats) I could imagine myself doing much the same with Richard had our circumstances not been easier. It did not comfort me to blame myself—was it my fault that she was making terrible mistakes? Richard thought it was. He would become angry whenever he saw Sarah and Bob together, and angry with me for not objecting more; when she ran off, he was furious. Where I think I may have been most mistaken was in not paying greater attention, not even believing, really, how angry Richard had become. For me, cold fear was stronger, and when Sarah did reappear, my relief and gratitude were so great I could not possibly have turned away from her.

The courtroom made me think I was in church, one of the milder, Protestant sort: a high, peaked ceiling of light polished wood; on one side, a raised desk the judge sat behind; on the other, banked seats for the jury, like a choir; for witnesses, a table and a couple of chairs arranged on a platform at the back of the room, resembling an altar. The rest of us sat facing the witness table, on pews of the same blonde wood. But the atmosphere was far from benign. The degree of animosity against Sarah on the part of the

SARAH

children's aunt—that she should go to all this trouble—shocks me yet. My own feelings toward the woman certainly included gratitude, that she had looked after Sarah's children when Sarah clearly had not, and Sarah had admired and trusted her at the same time as she refused my own offers of help. I sympathize, too, with her wanting to keep contact with the children (Ole, the older boy, has remained with her). But while Sarah had suggested a variety of compromises, the aunt would not consider any.

Testimony at the hearing caught me up on ten years of Sarah's life that I knew hardly anything about. Some was from very hostile witnesses, other from evidently warm friends, and all of it pretty much in agreement as to facts, if presenting a rather disorderly chronology. Sarah had left Bob and the farm when Ariel was six months old and moved into a house in Madison called Martha's Co-op, where she was said not to have done her share of work, and let her babies wander about in other people's care. The household sounded like a shabby collective end to the sixties' counterculture. Sarah had enrolled in a federally funded program in carpentry, and was able sometimes to pay rent by making repairs wherever she was living. For a while she went to West Virginia and had a tourist job running rapids in rubber boats—she had sent snapshots home of that adventure. One winter Ariel had stayed with his father in Madison, the two of them living pretty much in the car in the aunt's driveway. Ariel was spending a few days a week in each of three households (his father's car, the aunt's apartment, Martha's Co-op in care of a friend of Sarah's). How could Sarah not have known, I marveled, that children are not brought up by committee?

She was learning that now, having been living in Madison since August in a manner that I would consider exaggerated respectability in order to reestablish contact with her children and satisfy the court that she could care for them. She had rented an apartment, arranged shared time with the aunt for Ole and Ariel, was doing volunteer work at their elementary school, attending a parenting class, taking court-ordered psychological evaluation tests, and working at a bakery. And, she told me, she wrote every day to Richard, her husband, a carpenter in West Virginia, who, between visits to Madison, continued making furniture. Sarah was carrying on these various activities well, and there were teachers, co-workers, neighbors, and other friends in the courtroom willing to say so. They spoke of her good nature, her patience, and her ability in the school to get children to enjoy writing. She was "gentle" with them, a teacher said. A neighbor who had been involved in a volunteer project on behalf of abused children said that her son Jessie played with Ariel regularly after school, usually at Sarah's house. Ariel's music teacher called him a lively, "normal" little boy. I was glad to hear of Teresa, the owner of the bakery where Sarah worked. Visibly pregnant, Teresa told of Sarah's going with her to the hospital on the day she found out she was pregnant. For me, these were glimpses of a more familiar Sarah.

But other professionals had damaging (and jargon-ridden) evidence against her. In Sarah's apartment one afternoon, Ariel and Ole had invented a game of hanging each other. Ole reportedly turned blue, and his aunt was outraged enough to take him to the psychiatrist who had been appointed to the case. In court, the man said that what he called The Rope Incident was evidence that Sarah "lacked affect" because she had not reacted more strongly. The psychiatrist appeared angered by her calm. He disapproved of the fact that Sarah had merely talked with the boys, as she herself explained, and had not, what he termed, "imposed consequences" to punish them. He said that Ariel was suffering "cognitive withdrawal to a severe degree," evidently because, while Ariel attended a "rough" school, he did not engage in fights. The aunt and the psychologist also were holding it against her, Sarah told me, that only a few days after Ariel had first learned to ride alone on his bicycle, she and he had cycled the entire fifteen miles around the lake, Ariel returning exhausted but ecstatic. Clearly among other issues there were differing views of how one lived. Sarah was tolerating what others thought was somewhat strange behavior and encouraging adventurousness that did not measure well by more conventional standards. She showed me proudly Ariel's bed frame that he had helped her carpenter; by her account, he was the builder.

On Thursday morning, lawyers made their final arguments. Sarah's lawyer, whom I suspect was a little baffled by Sarah, acknowledged that facts were not in dispute: witnesses had not differed from Sarah's initial testimony. Sarah had indeed made many mistakes, her lawyer said, but that did not mean that she was not changing, nor that she was incapable of living with more stability. Her months in Madison, under closer scrutiny than most parents ever know, demonstrated her determination to take the best care she was able of Ariel. The time to have taken out court orders would better have been when Sarah was moving back and forth among California, West Virginia, and Madison, without ensuring care for Ariel, but not at the very moment when she began to be in a position to make a home for him, and was determined to do so. Whatever Sarah's mistakes in the past, the lawyer urged, the court ought to look to her better prospects in the future. Evidently the jury agreed, for two hours later they announced Sarah and Ariel could be together, or in court language, "the court should no longer have jurisdiction" over him.

Leaving the court building, Richard, Sarah, and I walked across the statehouse square. Spring was much farther along than in North Dakota—trees in leaf, tulips in bloom. We sat on a bench to eat the sandwiches we'd brought. A marching band in red uniforms came loudly up the street. Was this a holiday? Was there a game—football or basketball? None of us knew, but the band looked trim, untroubled, cheerfully patriotic. The world did seem to have taken a quarter-turn toward normalcy and happiness. I don't know whether I was more amazed or grateful. Ten years ago, I would not have thought I could look forward to merely being with Sarah; and to see her with Richard Sink, someone she cared for and who appeared to care for her, seemed a gift. People can change, life in small ways can get better. These are old revelations, and yet each time I hear that someone's life has taken a turn for the better, I can't help being freshly amazed, as though some grand wheel of fortune in the most frightful medieval woodcut had been bested. Of course this was not an entirely happy ending. Sarah and Richard and Ariel would return to West Virginia, but leave Ole behind and the brothers separated. It is Ole I worry about: bright yet strained. But the boys talk on the telephone, and Ole visits in West Virginia, and Sarah says each visit is easier.

There is so much in Sarah's life and way of living that I approve of, admire, and often envy. I recognize details from the way we lived when she was little. Yet sometimes it is as though she had misinterpreted something—I want to say Yes, but that was not quite the point—and it happens with all the children, whose present lives look cobbled from this or that piece of our past together. It must be an experience of all parents, the reverse of wanting to do differently than your own mother and father had, with similar materials. I doubt that in most instances you can really say one or another action was absolutely wrong in bringing up children, you can only suppose it might have been so after the fact, and the same "fact" can affect different children differently. Sarah appears to have been sustaining the frugal, abstemious household we lived with when the children were little, for she has had less to live on than Richard and I started out with. But I want to say to her that a comfortable chair or two and a good light to read by ought not compromise anyone's principles. The absence of comfortable chairs (but not the thick, polished deal tables and benches Richard and she have built) may hark back to the summer we lived in the farmhouse outside of Seattle when Richard had some leave from Ohio State and he and I finished our dissertations. Sarah would have been about five, Stephen three, and Andrew a year old. We lived with what we had

SARAH

brought as camping gear: Richard's army trunk was the coffee table, we sat on canvas camping stools or on the floor, and slept on air mattresses. A friend from graduate school came by one evening and asked Richard what was he going to do in real life, and we laughed that this *was* our real life. The setting was lovely—the house was to be demolished for a freeway, but had been built by Italians, and there was an apple orchard in back and fig trees espaliered against the west wall. There were two tall fir trees on either side of the front door.

Sarah and Stephen were still young enough to take naps and had been sent upstairs to bed one afternoon as usual. Richard and I were at our typewriters. Pretty soon Sarah and Stephen came in the front door and went upstairs, and some minutes later they did it again. I must have told them to stay in bed, and didn't think more of it. Then there was a knock at the door, and a man saying did we know that little children were climbing down the trees from an upstairs window? He had been watching them as he drove by on the highway. We had not noticed that their trips up the stairs had not been preceded by journeys down.

I think of episodes like that, and wonder whether the children could have interpreted their part of the experience as abandonment. Did some of them think they were not looked after? That while I was welcoming their developing independence and appreciating ingenuity even when it looked like mischief, they thought they were being left to fend for themselves? Because as I look back on twenty-some years of their collective childhoods, I do not remember a moment not being conscious of them, always keeping track, automatically reacting to them first, to any whimper in the night. Yet even when they climbed down the trees, I couldn't share our caller's alarm (embarrassed, I thanked him for his trouble). If Sarah and Stephen were managing to get down those trees, then it stood to reason they were able to do it without hurting themselves and were all right. That they were supposed to be in bed seemed a relatively minor point. I admired Sarah's not going wild, as some parents might have, when she discovered her sons playing at strangling each other. What I could not fathom was her turning them over to their aunt and other friends.

Apart from the dreadfulness of the hours in the courtroom, that visit in Madison was, as I've said, full of thankful discoveries. Sarah looked beautiful: athletic, calm-featured, an astonishment to me always. She told me that some days earlier when lawyers had taken depositions, she had cried, but the day before the actual hearing began, she had unnerved the same lawyers with her self-possession. I was not surprised, for she has always seemed to me to have had an almost uncanny dignity. She must have been about a year and a half when, in gray jumper with red rick-rack, she sat one day in Richard's St. Vincent de Paul leather chair, folded her hands, and said (nearly her first words), "Just like Daddy."

The basement in that Seattle farmhouse we lived in, a dying cherry orchard behind it, was nearly copied by Sarah's four rooms in Madison, with small porch on the second floor of a frame house. There were her loom, several beautifully wrought benches from Richard's workshop, brass rubbings she had brought from home, and her children's drawings on the walls. One afternoon from the upstairs porch I watched Sarah and Richard Sink and Ole throw a frisbee for the dog to leap at in flight, or retrieve when one of them missed, back and forth patiently in the small yard. Ole tired first and sat on a platform constructed in a lilac tree, the blossoms almost brushing the porch.

Now, several years from that spring in Madison, when I visit Sarah in West Virginia, we grow closer to the friends we used to be, when she was the eldest and would come into my room if I was lying on the bed reading. She'd bring her book along, both of us hiding away from the younger children. She and Richard and Ariel and two more baby boys live on a farm, four miles of hilly gravel roads from the workshop. And again, when Ariel is at school and

SARAH

the babies asleep, the two of us read, or make jam, or chat. There are two houses side by side on the farm. The family lives in one, and the other, smaller, Sarah has appropriated for herself, with the loom, spinning wheel, and her musical instruments. She has been weaving rugs and plans to sell rugs with chests that Richard makes. She knows women in the area who weave or spin or dye silk yarn, and takes me to visit them.

She awes me in her manner of tying together strands of her life. Michael Brady is the name Sarah and Richard Sink gave their first child, Brady for the Sioux Greek language major who appeared often in our house in Grand Forks, barefoot, to play with the children when they came home from school. I'd find him on the living room floor at cards, or constructing towers with building blocks. He was discovered dead one morning on the sidewalk near campus where he had been running, his heart enlarged with cancer. Sarah went to the funeral on the reservation. I hope that with a son named for him, she mourns Brady a little less.

On her farm when I visited one end of May, dogwood at the edge of clearings were in bloom, and up the road through the woods in a horse pasture I came upon a bathtub kept to overflowing by water from a pipe emerging from a spring. Underfoot were blossoming strawberries, clumps of blackberries and raspberries in the fields, and birds never stopped their racket. West Virginia is a poor state; Sarah tells me that 95 percent of coal mines are owned by people out of state who pay no taxes. But everywhere she took me made me think I was in a national park. I gave in entirely to that pastoral, familial setting. I read a little, wrote a few letters, and otherwise cooked and cleaned, hung out laundry, planted beans that mysteriously came up in a week, went for walks, and dandled babies. Rolland, the six-month-old, would be lying in a wagon, and Michael, at two, walking alongside as we trudged the hillside road. A turtle crossed in front of us, its bright marking so like Chinese characters I thought if only I knew Chinese I should be able to read them. Another morning it was a caterpillar in our path, its legs moving in successive waves of equally bright yellow. We paused, Rolland's head bobbing now and then above the side of the wagon, and Michael gazing apprehensively, thumb in mouth and the other hand holding the elbow. Michael told his mother one evening when I was cooking supper that he was going in to "help Ma-gro-ther" (pronouncing every syllable with equal force). That family needs a magrother, I told them—full time—and for a couple of weeks I was glad to provide the office. Sarah, meanwhile, would be hauling wheelbarrow loads of manure up the steep rocky drive to her vegetable garden, picking out rocks, planting and tending.

Sarah reminds me more and more of Mother, and I catch myself feeling with her the way I did with Mother—wanting to be friends, a little wary, accommodating myself to her habits, I daresay even hoping for approval. Sarah looks like Mother; she is not as tall, and she is healthier and more athletic, but her dark hair, high cheekbones, and way of moving shyly into a group make me think of Mother. Mother made a favorite out of her when she was little, sending smocked dresses that were beautiful though far out of style for the tie-dyed sixties. When I'd be with Mother, home from school or college, and doing a flurry of catch-up work about the ranch—painting, sewing, mending, berry-picking—it would distress me that she seemed to sit around playing solitaire and say she was tired all the time. And with Sarah, who danced ballet in her early teens and now is developing considerable talent in weaving, I hold back my compulsion to tell her to get on with it, not bury herself in laundry and dirty dishes, still trying from both to learn a less driven pace for myself.

It pleases me especially to think of a small tie between the two of them. My father bought a pearl necklace for one hundred dollars from a Jew leaving Germany, and had given the pearls to Mother at the time I was born. The necklace was to be mine when I reached eighteen, but she might wear it in the meantime. She did, often, and long after I was eighteen. I wore it just once myself, when Mother put it on me at my wedding, because I could never bring myself to explain to my parents that its representing a family's escape from certain death was more than I could bear around my neck. I brought the pearls in their blue leather case away with me only after Mother died. Sarah has them now, and was wearing the necklace when she sat in the courtroom, as lovely as ever Mother looked—a good omen, I hoped, of flight to a new beginning.

ABOUT THE AUTHOR

ELIZABETH HAMPSTEN lives in Grand Forks and teaches English at the University of North Dakota. From 1981 to 1989 she edited the magazine *Plainswoman*. She is the author of *Read This Only to Yourself: Writings of Midwestern Women 1880–1910* (Indiana University Press, 1982) and *Settler Children: Growing Up On the Great Plains* (University of Oklahoma Press, 1991).